PRAISE FOR GET

"It's not often that you read a s[...] emotionally, involves you in real personal situations, and takes you back to the basics along the way. Highly recommended—it provides an actionable game plan."

Harry Buckel
Chairman, Maryland Pennysaver Group

"As a sales professional in the hospitality industry, I am faced with potential wipeouts every day. This book is just the ignition I was looking for to get *my* desire, drive, and determination out of the whitewater and position myself as a big-wave sales rider! I recommend this book to all my colleagues in sales. Grab this book, kick off the flipflops, and enjoy the ride!"

Michelle Crosby, CMP, DMCP
Senior Sales Manager, Ultimate Adventures

"In this book Eloise Owens chronicles her discovery of surfing, and surfing's best, including the Willis brothers, as a source of incredible inspiration for sales and for life."

Catherine J. Mackey, Ph.D.
Senior Vice President, Pfizer Global Research and Development
Director, La Jolla Laboratories

"As a top salesperson I thought I had it down to a science . . . but then I read this book. Just when you think you are the *best*, there's always room for improvement, and this wonderful read will make you regroup, refocus, and rethink! Being the top salesperson year after year doesn't always assure me I am going to stay on top and after reading this book, I now know that I never catch just any wave, but strive toward catching the monster waves! This book left me wanting higher waves!"

Jodye Newton
Senior Account Executive, Star-Telegram

"*Get off the Beach!* is a fun book with a serious message about how to sell more and enjoy the process. This creative blend of surfing and selling techniques will inspire and equip you."

Mark Sanborn
Author, You Don't Need a Title to Be a Leader

"Gnarly!! The surf's up around our office with the super sales (and life) lessons from Eloise's latest book. The message is clear and cool: Love what you do and those who help you do it, and the smooth ride will be the best reward. *Get off the Beach!* will entice even the most staid salesperson to jump in the water and ride monster waves!"

Charles W. Northern, CIC
President, Risk Services of Louisiana LLC

"After nearly fifteen years of sales and sales management, I have seen the pretenders. This book, like every visit from Eloise, manages to reach out to the veteran as well as the rookie. Eloise always manages to reinforce the positive, gently nudge the bad habits, and leave you wanting more. This book is the same combination. Basic enough for the rookies and advanced enough to challenge the most talented veterans."

Stacey Ream
Advertising Director, Freedom Communications, Inc.

"Eloise is a true professional. She knows sales and understands salespeople. This book captures perfectly how salespeople can kick it up a notch in their selling careers and stay on top . . . it's all about momentum!"

Jonathan J. Theophilakos
Director of Advertising, Greater Media Newspapers

"Selling is like surfing? Who knew? Eloise Owens does, and the lessons she shares will give you confidence and commitment to ride big waves."

Randy Pennington
Author, Results Rule!

"Sales is a challenging profession, but Eloise helps you meet those challenges in a most unique way. *Get off the Beach!* is a must-read for any sales or sales management professional who's ready for higher waves of success!"

Laura Bader
Vice President Advertising and Sales Development,
Tribune Company

"After one of my most successful quarters as a software account executive, I found myself languishing on the beach. I was hesitant to take some of the chances and make some of the efforts that had made me successful in the past. Reading *Get off the Beach!* motivated me to chase the big waves again. As a result, this year will be the largest income I have ever achieved in my fifteen-year sales career. Thanks, Eloise!"

Mike Moore
Software Account Executive, SAP America

"A marvelous integration of talent, knowledge, and inspiration for every competitive professional and leader. *Get off the Beach!* will inspire you to act, enjoy, and thrive in your life."

Erick Schick
CEO, Pantheon

"This is a sales masterpiece. Eloise guides you through all the dynamics of relational understanding in a way that leaves you wanting more. It gives you life skills that transcend the traditional sales methods. This book helps you realize the freedom to step back and start over with a refreshed sense of purpose."

Jeff Noble
Advertising Director, The Beaumont Enterprise

"I started reading this book wondering how the heck surfing related to selling, and before I knew it I was caught up in the wave of the challenges of both surfers and salespeople—wonderful comparisons. I thoroughly enjoyed reading each and every word."

Donna M. Lundborg
Director of Marketing, On Call Home Care

"Learn where effort and execution meet. A must-read to build your momentum and keep it!"

Michael Christopher
Customer Relationship Manager, Concentra Health Services

"While *Get off the Beach!* focuses on improving sales team results, these great concepts can be applied to anyone who wants to increase their effectiveness. Really enjoyed the book."

Kathleen Hamilton
President, US Subsidiary, Electro Medical Systems Corp.

"Every sales organization needs momentum. Eloise's new book, *Get off the Beach!*, teaches you how to build your sales momentum by aligning your actions and thoughts for waves of continued success! Get ready ... you will love this book!"

Betty Carr
Group Publisher, Vice President,
Metroland Printing, Publishing, and Distributing, Ltd.

"Great sellers earn the right to 'ride the high wave' of success. Eloise has captured the life tools for every seller to be *on* that wave peak. Read her and ride high."

Bob Danzig
Former CEO Hearst Newspapers; Author-Speaker

GET OFF THE BEACH!

What Legendary Surfers Know
That Salespeople
Need to Know...Now

Krista –
Here's to higher
waves!
Eloise

GET OFF THE BEACH!

What Legendary Surfers Know
That Salespeople
Need to Know...Now

ELOISE OWENS

Eloise

J. P. HARRIS PUBLISHING

GET OFF THE BEACH!

© 2006 Eloise Owens

Published by J.P. Harris Publishing
601 Van Ness, Suite 148
San Francisco, California 94102

www.momentumcompany.com

All rights reserved. No portion of this book may be reproduced, stored in a retrieval system, or transmitted in any form or by any means— electronic, mechanical, photocopy, recording, or any other—except for brief quotations in printed reviews, without prior permission of the publisher.

Edited by Patty Crowley
Cover design by Jim Weems
Interior design by Inside Out Design & Typesetting

ISBN: 978-0-9789321-0-7
ISBN: 0-9789321-0-2

Printed in the United States of America
2006—First Edition

10 9 8 7 6 5 4 3 2

This book is proudly dedicated to my two redheads,

Tyler Owens, for teaching me to see through the eyes of an artist.

It has humbled me.

Benay Owens, for your absolute faith in me.

It inspires me.

My life wouldn't be nearly as much fun

without you two in it.

Love unending.

Tyler Owens

Benay Owens

CONTENTS

Contents

GRATITUDE TO MY
WAVE WARRIORS

Acknowledgments

Thanks to my book muse and forever mentor, Bette Price. To Gary Rifkin and Christine Cashen for living the adventure with me. To Linda Swindling . . . here's to crazy ideas, huh?

Kudos to my readers, who pushed me to tell it like it is: Bill Dragoo, Brian Landreth, Jason Jacoby, Brent Erdman, Jeff Conley, Stacey Ream, Jodye Newton, Doug Smart, Greg Godek, Rick Alexander, Eric Schick, and to Mikey, who keeps me laughing and true to myself.

Thanks to my band of friends who were willing to share their expertise and stories to bring *Get off the Beach!* to life: Philip Mosakowski, Roger Fallows, Butch Owens, Kevin, Linda Thomas, Allen Tappe, Jeff Conley, Randy Gage, Mike Hoffman, Jonathan Naizer, Chris Clarke Epstein, Martin Brazil, and Smokey Garrett.

Thanks to my surf family:

McCall, the "eyes" still have it.

Acknowledgments

Dana, for your hospitality and mangoes at midnight.

Gene and Sandra Willis, welcoming this Texan into your home.

Brooks, to our backyard adventures.

Terry Lamb, for your artistic eyes.

Sanami, for your gentle surfer spirit.

Jason, for barbeque brownies.

Lori and Joe, for my wonderful "casita."

Patty, who I met at the Mavericks' surf gift shop. You still inspire me by your determination to surf higher waves of success despite those pesky wipeouts.

Thanks to my Momentum clients: Sandy Theo, Tom Eason, Jeff Noble, Laura Bader, Gene Villarreal, Darwin Oordt, Harry Buckel, Stacey Ream, Matt Chisler, John Derr, Wes Turner, and Mike Winter for all your trust and confidence in allowing me to make waves with your sales teams. I am blessed to work with such great leaders.

Applause for all my National Speakers Association colleagues, including David Rich, Max Jaffe, Al Lucia, Susan Gatton, Randy Pennington, Vince Poscente, Sam Horn, Tim Durkin, and so many others who kept me moving forward when I became a weary writer.

Thanks to my family:

My sisters, Mary, Linda, Maggie, and my mom, Ruth.

Thank you for being my cheerleaders, now that we are an all-girl team!

To my dad, who is selling books in heaven at this very moment. Thank you for your love of selling. I miss you every day.

To my editors and designers who worked their magic to help me find the best words and limit the exclamation points:

Patty Crowley, for encouraging and polishing my voice.

Gary Rifkin, for sharpening my voice.

Ann Baird, for organizing my voice.

Bette Price, for the patience to let me discover my own voice.

Kathryn Murray, for designing my voice.

Jim Weems, for wrapping the cover bow around my voice.

Foremost, gratitude to God, who lays adventures at our feet every day. Thank you for all of them, especially this one.

Special thanks to Milton and Michael Willis — two surfers who taught me more about life and selling from the wisdom of the waves. Your surfboard proudly hangs in my office as a reminder of the power of unlikely intersections and perfect days.

FOREWORD

Go Big!

Living up to your full potential and becoming a good surfer are easy if you know how, nearly impossible if you don't. Everyone has the potential to become a great surfer, a great salesperson, or great at anything you desire to be. But first and foremost you must possess or attain accurate knowledge. You may have all the desire or hope in the world, but without accurate knowledge, success in any endeavor, big or small, becomes a guessing game of chance at best.

Big-wave surfers are made, not born. Every big-wave surfer, at one time or another, had a guide, an experienced teacher, someone knowledgeable who helped show the way. In the world of big-wave sales, Eloise Owens shares her vast and profound insights showing others the way to real and long-lasting success.

In surfing, it's not always easy to get off the beach and into the waves, especially when the waves are fifty feet or more. But with clear desire, heartfelt commitment, and applied accurate knowledge, believe me, it can be done.

In her book *Get off the Beach!* Eloise Owens draws a brilliant correlation between surfing success and sales success that everyone, not just surfers and salespeople, can benefit from. Eloise Owens shares the valuable secrets of her sales success your competition does not want you to know. She shares top secrets such as how to get into the sales flow, find and create sales momentum, and achieve successful results.

Know this: every surfer has the ability to ride big waves; few, however, will ever accomplish such feats. Likewise, every person in sales has a chance to go big; few, however, will. It's not that they cannot or do not want to; it's just that they do not know how. Many are paralyzed with thoughts of wiping out or failure, when all along success is right there waiting to be taken. If you know what to do, you can do it!

Big-wave surfers have a saying: "Do not rely on luck when you can rely on knowledge." They stack the odds of success in their favor. To stack the odds of success in your favor you do not need luck, just a copy of Eloise Owens' book. So go big, live to your full potential, become one of the few who do.

There is no wave too big, no wave too small. Catch the
wave of success—it's the best wave of all.
—MICHAEL WILLIS AND
MILTON WILLIS

INTRODUCTION

Welcome to the Adventure

Have you ever experienced a friend giving you an idea that you knew was a bit crazy? We were brainstorming one day in my office about book ideas and my friend Linda came up with a doozie. "Since your company logo is an ocean wave, what if you interviewed surfers and used surfing analogy to help salespeople sell more?" she suggested. I politely smiled and thought, *That's the dumbest idea I've ever heard.* True, surfers were again starting to become popular in our American culture, but I was a middle-aged mother of two, living in landlocked Dallas, Texas. What would I know about surfing? I thanked my friend for her "great idea" and the next week headed to speak in beautiful La Jolla, California. Hey, somebody has to go, right?

Longing for the ocean breeze on my face, I opted to sit

outside at a local restaurant and ordered a great California sandwich. You know, the kind with avocado and alfalfa sprouts on it. Waiting for my sandwich to arrive, I glanced over and saw the local newspaper, the *La Jolla Light*, sitting on the iron patio table to my right. I grabbed it and began thumbing through it. It was a tabloid-sized newspaper with all the latest area happenings and stories from local contributors. It was a refreshing change of pace from reading my more traditional *Dallas Morning News*.

There on page 18 was a title that caught my eye: "Life and Surfing" by Milton and Michael Willis. The article was an intriguing one. These two surf brothers were using their surfing expertise to write about life lessons, and I found that, for a couple of surfer dudes, their insights were quite impressive. Just then, my sandwich arrived. After taking the first bite of my turkey-Swiss-avocado-alfalfa-sprouts-on-whole-wheat cool California sandwich, I couldn't stop reading the article. My mind raced back to my friend's suggestion and I giggled at the thought that maybe, just maybe, her idea wasn't so crazy after all.

You don't have to hit me with a ton of bricks for me to get the irony of the timing here. Within one week, a brainstorming session on a surf idea, then an intriguing life lessons article from surfers. I ripped out their article from the newspaper, tucked it in my briefcase, and decided to contact the surfers when I returned home.

I know, on the surface, selling and surfing might seem to have little in common.

I know, on the surface, selling and surfing might seem to have little in common. That's what I thought a few years ago. Today, this book has proved that idea wrong, again and again.

In the chapters to come, you'll meet Michael and Milton along with other professional surfers who were challenged to redefine their sport and take it to impossible levels. You'll meet big-wave riders who understand the importance of total commitment and inner strength in the face of incredible odds; surfers who bring a love and passion to their sport that impacts people all around them.

At times throughout this book you will be immersed into their surfing world, yet if you're like me, fresh sales lessons will also be leaping off the pages. As salespeople, we all need fresh ideas, new perspectives to rekindle our drive to achieve. Why? Because we are in a crazy business! Think about it. We walk into businesses, pick up telephones, send e-mails, and prepare presentations all in the hopes of finding the yes's amidst the sea of no's. Chances are, the prospects didn't ask for interruptions and most likely feel they have better things to do with their day than to let you persuade them to "yes."

We've been rejected, interrupted, embarrassed, frustrated, and at times, disappointed in the pursuit of that "yes." Now, here's the crazy part . . . we get up the next day and do it all over again. Come on, don't you have nonsales friends who look at you like a dog staring at a ceiling fan? They just don't get your sales world and how you can do it year after year. But here's

When the "no" turns to "yes," well, it just ROCKS!

what they don't get and maybe never will: selling rocks!

When our product or service provides a solution for our customer's needs and they get results, it rocks! When we build relationships that generate trust and mutual respect, that rocks! When we are able to feed that competitive fire that burns in many of us and be financially rewarded along the way, we rock! When the "no" turns to "yes," well, it just rocks! Sorry, but your nonsales friends will never really understand this craziness. But that's okay. This book is not for them—it is for you, the crazy salesperson.

I want to invite you on a crazy adventure, where sales lessons are waiting in the most unusual places by people you'd least expect—big-wave professional surfers. These men and women who walk on water will enlighten you, challenge you, and motivate you. They will change you. They sure changed me.

The truth is, I never chose to write this book. It chose me. This adventure has brought countless lessons to my life, and I am humbled to share them with you. I am different today because of what I've learned. I hope you will be too.

As expert surfers will tell you, you can't get good at surfing by staring at the waves and wishing. In spite of fear, angst, and hesitation, if you want to catch higher waves of success, you must first get in the water. So . . . *let's get off the beach!*

Surf's up . . . get off the beach!

From: Eloise Owens
Subject: Interview
To: Willis Brothers
Sent: 2/6/03

I was recently in your beautiful city and saw your surfing article in the newspaper. I am writing a sales book using surfer quotes and perspectives and am amazed at the similarities of your sport and my profession of selling. The newspaper was kind enough to give me your e-mail address. Please let me know if you would be willing to be interviewed.

Sincerely,

Eloise Owens

1
SURF'S UP, SALES UP

Mastering Sales Momentum

I had no idea when I hit the Send button on my computer that my e-mail would land in the inbox of two of Hawaii's surfing legends, now living in Southern California. It was a simple request, really.

Within minutes, my phone rang. His voice was pure surfer, filled with excitement at the possibilities of my idea. We talked for an hour, awkwardly asking questions about each other's world, until it slowly started to sink in just who these surfer dudes really were.

I had read about these guys who surfed the first "Condition Black" in Hawaii in the late 1990s. "Condition

Black" means that ocean conditions are so treacherous that people are cleared off the beaches. That day the beaches did clear, except for eight big-wave riders. Two of them were now on the other end of my telephone — Michael and his twin brother, Milton.

The longer they spoke, the more I was amazed. Big-wave riders have much to teach us sales folk. I could sense there were many lessons to learn, but right then, my stomach was starting to churn. A thousand thoughts raced through my mind. What was their expertise going to cost me? These guys are some of the best in their field . . . at the pinnacle of their sport . . . the rock stars of surfing. Surely, they weren't going to let me interview them for free!

Michael then graciously spoke. "We would love to help you in any way we can — on one condition."

I grimaced and thought, "I knew it! Here it comes; the dollar signs."

Michael continued, "Come to California and let us show you how to surf. Eloise, you can't write about what you don't know."

Whaaaat? I was stunned! Visions of tsunami waves and twenty-year-olds in bikinis flashed before my eyes. (I'm not sure which one was more threatening.)

Laughing out loud I replied, "You're kidding, right?" He wasn't laughing. All of a sudden, paying them for the interview seemed like the better deal.

Surfing has taken Hollywood by storm! Advertisers are hitting the beach, with surfers selling everything from cars to cell phones. It seems the marketplace can't get enough of surfers. But if you think that big-wave riders are just dudes whose great tans replaced their IQs, think again. The hit movie *Blue Crush*, as well as the 2005 opening picture at Sundance Film Festival, *Riding Giants*, showcased men and women with a rare inner fortitude, focus, and full-hearted commitment to surf higher and faster than ever thought possible. We should all be so dumb.

On the surface, selling and surfing might seem to have little in common. That's what I thought, at first. Oh, was I wrong. They actually have a lot in common.

Selling is a blend of intellect, skill, and instinct. So is surfing. Both demand passion, and both offer the potential for wipeouts every day. But most importantly, sales and surfing share a common element needed to achieve success and to stay at the top of the game: Momentum! Surfers ride it. Salespeople create it.

A NEW KIND OF MOMENTUM

Were you paying attention in physics class? Well, neither was I. But from the little science I do remember from high school, *momentum* is defined as "mass in motion" or "mass times velocity." The amount of momentum an object has is dependent upon two variables: (1) how much stuff is moving (mass) and (2) how fast the stuff is moving (velocity). This word *momentum* refers to the amount of motion that an object has. So an object that has momentum is on the move and is going to take some effort to stop. But an object that has tremendous momentum is really on the move and virtually impossible to stop.

For salespeople, momentum is the degree of energy we have moving us toward our goals. I call it *sales momentum*. The more sales momentum we have, the greater the energy we have toward our goals and the harder it is for us to be stopped. It is an energy that helps us break through obstacles, rethink opportunities, and keep us energized.

So why is this energy force in such limited supply in so many sales careers? Or is it? As a sales coach I have observed firsthand the answer to that question. Creating and sustaining momentum isn't easy. And, as humans, we love "easy," don't we? There's nothing easy about momentum, but it can be created. Before we look at creating momentum, we need to first look at some universal truths.

Momentum is the degree of energy we have moving us toward our goals.

Momentum Is Not Your Friend

All of us at times have been guilty of taking our friends for granted, haven't we? We get so comfortable that we stop doing the things we know our friends like and appreciate. Momentum is no different. I've seen sales reps who have walked across the stage winning national sales awards, and within months have plummeted out of their company's top tier of salespeople. What happened? They probably stopped doing the things that built their momentum and subsequently paid the price with lower results. Okay, the truth is, that was me! Has it been you, too?

Momentum Is a Diva

If you think J. Lo is high maintenance, get ready for this energy diva! She demands your undivided attention. She doesn't care about what you did last year. She just cares about what you have done for her lately. This diva dines on caviar, wears Prada, and drives a Porsche, baby! Only the best for her! She demands the best out of you, too. Be attentive to her and she'll be attentive to you; but if you try and give less than your best, she'll dump you faster than you can say, "Trust me." Loyalty is not exactly her strong suit. Hey, she's a diva!

Momentum Hates Routine

It's our ruts and routines that we so easily fall into that cause momentum to weaken. Doing the unexpected, however, gives momentum room to work for you. I have interviewed top sales professionals in various industries who have accelerated their momentum through the ability to create the unexpected. Salespeople who look at their territories as a land of endless opportunities waiting to be discovered, who won't settle for no's, creatively find a better way to create more yes's instead.

These truths aren't easy. We wrestle with them—just like surfers do.

The Surfer's Truth

Surfing Hawaii's monster wave commonly known as Jaws seemed impossible—a definite surfer's "no." Picture a body of water the height of a twenty-story building with enough power to flip a locomotive like a toy. *Outside* magazine describes it this way: "Jaws: Those who know it best—fear it most!" For years, surfers could only watch Jaws from the shore, with the ground rumbling beneath their feet. Some of those brave souls who ventured out paid the ultimate price.

Truth is, the surfers' arms were not strong enough and their surfboards were not equipped to navigate the monster waves. The problem was, they couldn't generate enough speed to master the momentum of the wave or to get ahead of the monster wave to surf it. These obstacles were just too big and sent them back to the beach where it was safe and sane.

The Salesperson's Truth

I have stood on that beach. Haven't you? You know, facing monster sales goals, wondering how in the world you're going to hit your numbers again . . . this year. Like you, I've found myself dealing with frustrations of a manager who puts up more roadblocks than she clears yet still needs you to produce higher results . . . again. Or you feel smothered by the waves of paperwork that never seem to go away. Then you internalize the overwhelming pressure of sales goals that keep rising, while your sales energy to meet those goals evaporates. Standing on that beach staring at the sales waves ahead can be exhausting. I remember hearing that little voice inside my head that whispered, *Are you equipped? Are you strong enough? Can you pull it off again this year?*

I was an average salesperson, lumped in the middle of the pack of sales performers for the company where

Standing on that beach staring at the sales waves ahead can be exhausting.

I worked. Some years were okay and some weren't. Sound familiar? Sales momentum wasn't exactly my best friend.

Watching the same top sales performers walk across the stage each year, heralded by the company as their best of the best, stirred a deep frustration in me. Sure, I applauded the winners on the outside, but I resented their success on the inside. I wanted to be on that stage. But the monster waves were just too high. What more could I do? The answer for me was easy—just keep doing more of the same and hope for better results! I had gotten too comfortable with my accounts, had held back giving my best, and had fallen into routines that clouded the opportunities right in front of me. All of these are common symptoms of low momentum and can lead to inconsistent results.

Salespeople need more momentum to ride higher sales waves, just like those surfers stuck on the safe beach who needed to get off the beach to ride the waves they longed for. They had to find a new way to ride momentum.

A Simple Idea to Harness Momentum

It was a small contingent of surfers who finally found the momentum answer to navigating monster waves like Jaws. With one simple new idea—adding a sail to their surfboards—these never-give-up surfers got the wind they needed to generate just enough forward energy to ride monster waves and take their sport to new and unstoppable levels. They conquered the monster waves by adding just one new idea, but that one idea generated a whole new level of momentum.

Another contingent of surfers, including Laird Hamilton, pioneered another new technique in the late 1990s, called tow-in surfing. With tow-in surfing the surfer is towed into a breaking wave by a partner driving a personal watercraft. Surfers need a tow-in when the wave is too large and moving too quickly for surfers to catch it by paddling with their hands or where position on the wave is extremely critical. Both are examples of creating momentum when it appears that no progress can be made.

You may never jump up on a surfboard for an epic surf day. But if you are a sales professional who has been standing on the beach gazing at monster waves, you need what big-wave riders use to master the momentum of monster waves—new ideas! This book is full of them. As you read on you'll find countless momentum-building ideas to inspire you to catch higher waves of success, get more sales, and enjoy your ride.

The surfers mastered momentum, and it changed their sport. Now it's your turn.

It's time to get off the beach!

As spring transformed into another hot Texas summer, the Willis brothers' invitations to join them in Southern California grew increasingly louder. I wish I could tell you that I heard a voice from the heavens, like Moses on the mountain, that said, "Go surf!" Oh, how I just wanted to hear a voice. The only voices I did hear were

from my two teenagers who thought their mom had lost her mind!

"Okay, Mom, let us get this straight. You are going to a place you've never been, to meet with two guys you don't know, to go try something that involves standing on a moving board . . . in the ocean . . . in a bathing suit?" The absurdity in their tone was not lost on me!

If I could just hear that guiding voice! Then on July 11, 2003, I finally heard it: "Now boarding American Airlines flight 1439 to San Diego." So I boarded the plane.

The waves are calling.

2

GET OUT OF THE

WHITEWATER

The Power of Self-Management

At last we meet! There in the driveway of the corporate headquarters of WB Surfing stood the man (or should I say the dude). It was Michael Willis, both hands outstretched, grinning from ear to ear. "Welcome to the adventure, Eloise Owens."

I recognized that surfer voice instantly and was happy to put a face to it — a tan face I might add. Instantly, I regretted skipping the tanning salon!

Michael stood not much taller than me, maybe five ten, a slight, taught frame, and not a hint of fat. We first shook hands, and then he gestured toward the corporate offices to invite me in. As we reached the office, actually a converted garage, there appeared surfer dude number two, Michael's twin brother, Milton, leaning against the side of their boat, parked in the driveway. Another bronze body in perfect shape. Milton gave me a warm aloha hug and welcomed me to Solana Beach. I quickly learned that Milton is the hugger; Michael not so much. Milton's warmth of welcome was followed closely by a quiet curiosity to find out more about me and why I had come.

I sensed that Milton knew I was a bit nervous, and he asked if I wanted to sit down. They offered me a chair, a milk crate, actually. And there, outside WB Surfing headquarters, sitting under a giant eucalyptus tree on a balmy day in July were two surfers and a saleswoman, silently wondering about an adventure that was about to unfold.

Waves don't just happen, they are created by a catalyst, something that makes a change happen or brings about an event. Common wave-creating catalysts include wind, earthquakes, or underwater disturbances. These catalysts give birth to waves ranging from small, tight ripples to massive tsunami waves that can move with the speed of a 747 jetliner. The bigger the catalyst, the grander the momentum, or forward energy, that runs through the water to give waves their power.

As salespeople, we have a catalyst as well. It influences our sales momentum and impacts our results. It is often overlooked and is easy to miss, if we're not careful.

THE SALES CATALYST AND THE STORY OF TRACEY

No amount of technique training, by itself, will consistently move the needle upward in sales performance and sustain a salesperson's momentum. That's the mistake one company almost made with their sales rep Tracey. I knew better.

Tracey, with her high-sales technique, should have been in her company's upper tier of sales achievers. But she wasn't. She was about to be fired when I got the call from my client.

They assumed that her low sales performance was a technique issue. Not necessarily. It's a common mistake both managers and salespeople make.

The same is true for surfers. If learning a technique is all it takes, then why aren't there hundreds and hundreds of big-wave surfers in the world going after the ultimate eighty-foot waves? That's easy. Not all surfers have what it takes to be big-wave riders regardless of the techniques they learn. In fact, on that epic surf day in 1998, only eight surfers chose to go! More than the surfing mechanics was at stake when they faced those monster waves. Now Tracey, like the surfers, needed to face her own waves. Yet with all the sales expertise in the world, she was simply stuck, standing on the beach.

Tracey had been through the company's sales training program, and her manager couldn't find anything wrong with her sales technique in the field. They asked me to come in and give her some coaching to see if there was any hope of getting her sales numbers up. We scheduled a meeting for the end of the week.

I had a hunch about Tracey as I walked into the conference room. I had been Tracey myself more than once in my twenty-five-year sales career, going through the motions with no real obvious sales performance gaps. I knew the craft of selling, much like I imagined Tracey did. Her problem—she had no momentum. Tracey did not need to learn more selling skills; she needed to discover the catalyst to jumpstart her momentum. Boy, did she ever.

Fast-forward with me to find Tracey twelve months later. The envelope is unsealed; the name is read for National Sales

Rep Runner Up. You guessed it—Tracey jumped from her chair and leaped to the stage to receive her award! She nearly tackled me as I waited offstage to congratulate her. Tracey got off the beach; she became a big-wave rider!

Tracey simply needed to rediscover the catalyst for her momentum—the power of self-management—the commitment to making it happen!

Were you hoping for a sexier answer? Most people do. Sorry. There isn't one; just the tough truth. You can never catch higher waves of success without developing a strong commitment to self-manage every facet of your sales career! And it's just as true for surfers.

Ever since Milton and Michael were young boys, they believed they were born to ride big waves. So they moved to Hawaii, determined to find the best waves and fulfill their quest.

They studied the ocean until it became a part of them. Physically, they conditioned and improved their body strength. They became world-renowned surfboard builders, creating their own Phazer model, crafted to handle the monster-size waves they longed to ride. They knew no one was going to hand them their dream; they themselves would have to make it happen. Self-management.

Welcome to the heartbeat of this book. Every single concept in this book will bring you only halfhearted results in your selling career unless you totally grasp the connection between creating momentum and your ability to manage your emotions, activities, and mindset. You and your commitment to self-management will determine your future ability to ride higher waves of success.

SALES WAVES

Tracey didn't win the National Sales Runner Up award by learning a better sales technique. She won by making a personal commitment to surf a different sales wave!

Let's look at three levels of sales waves by the degree of momentum that is flowing through them and how our ability to self-manage is the key to riding higher waves of success!

Wave Level 1: Whitewater Momentum

This size wave is at the lowest level because it has the smallest amount of energy, or momentum, running through it. These waves are close to the shore and safe. For surfers, whitewater waves are great for learning but not for improving skill. These smaller waves, because of their low momentum, aren't very long lasting thus do very little to help develop the surfer's advanced skills.

Salespeople who operate in whitewater waves also share the challenges of maneuvering in these low-energy waves.

Although risk is low at this level, success is tentative. While some victories can occur at this level, they will be short-lived.

Here are some examples of salespeople's whitewater victories:

- ❖ You are given an account list predominantly comprised of established customers. You have basically inherited your momentum.

- ❖ You leave a company and take your clients with you to begin selling them a new product line or service. This is often true of direct-selling companies. New product line, same customers: instant momentum.

- ❖ You wait for the phone to ring and celebrate the victory when you close the sale. Wait a minute . . . What's wrong with closing the sale and celebrating? Nothing. It's good practice for you. It's a victory when you're in whitewater!

What is common in the low-momentum, whitewater victories listed above? You guessed right if you said that they all involve an external condition, something you are hoping for or waiting on to happen. Not much self-management is needed for these waves. Don't get me wrong, I'll take the sales generated from each of these examples. But what if your established account list diminishes (they always do) or this time your customers don't want to change products (they won't) or the phone stops ringing (it will!)? You are not self-managing your momentum; you are order-taking at best, waiting for your momentum! Small waves, low momentum equal short-term results!

Momentum does not reward you long-term when you depend on the externals.

Momentum does not reward you long-term when you depend on the externals and let someone or something determine your results. The success ride can be very short. Whitewater victories are ultimately painful for salespeople who are addicted to externals for their results. I know. I personally have felt that pain.

I cringe at the memory of a meeting with my district manager, Julie, many years ago. My stomach hurts as I relive this story. The company had increased my sales goals one year, and I was fuming! I finished number seven in the nation that year, and I felt I had earned the right to express my opinions. I marched—not walked, mind you—into my district manager's office and informed her that if she wanted to get this amount of production out of me, they were going to have to change a few things. Yikes, I think I even pointed my finger at her. I demanded that they must first expand my territory or at least switch me into a bigger one. I was convinced there was no way to generate this new amount of sales production out of my existing territory. Second, the sales materials we were using were soooo outdated. I insisted that they invest in upgrading our sales materials or forget about increasing sales. Last, and most important, the manager who they hired for our franchise office had to go! All of us in the office had lost all respect for her. She wasn't as good a salesperson as we were. We needed a better manager who understood us and could motivate us! *Humph!*

My district manager leaned back in her black, leather chair, her hands laced together behind her head. An emerging, most irritating smile came across her face. She was astute enough to recognize whitewater thinking when she heard it, and she was hearing it from me in surround sound!

I was an external addict! All three of my demands— territory change, updated sales materials, and a better manager—were my fix! If you just give them to me, I will be great and hit my numbers!

Ever thought about your list? I have a hunch I am not alone. In fact, I know I'm not. Now, as a sales coach, I've been sitting in many a sales manager's office when Peter,

Paul, or Mary comes marching in with their finger pointing and their demands emerging. It tells me instantly where they are surfin' . . . they're in the whitewater!

Self-management doesn't rely on the externals, and my manager had her hands full with me that day. I will never forget when that smile went away from her face. She leaned toward me in her nice leather chair and with a "thundering, velvet hand," changed my selling career forever! She helped me face my addiction . . . to say good-bye to the whitewater! She had become a great teacher for me with many lessons I needed to learn. More on Julie to come.

Wave Level 2: The Outside Waves

Eventually, it's time for the surfer to move to the "outside," where the waves build and break outside the whitewater.

She helped me face my addiction . . . to say good-bye to the whitewater!

These waves give surfers a better opportunity to hone their abilities and enjoy a longer ride. The size of outside waves can range anywhere from six to twelve feet. It is here on the outside waves that surfers spend most of their water time. When you move up to this level, the speed of the ride changes, because there is more energy running through the water, thus more momentum is carrying you.

At this point, the basics of surfing are being instilled into muscle memory, and surfers learn to execute more on instinct. This is where surfers develop their style, gain experience handling different wave sets, and learn to respect the ways of the water.

For a salesperson who navigates on the outside waves, the ride begins to change as well. You don't wait for the phone to ring; you make it ring. You get your toes wet in the world of being proactive, and self-management begins to take root. Here on the outside waves you have the fundamentals of selling instilled in you. You learn the basics of building rapport, uncovering needs, making a solid sales presentation, and helping your customers choose. You learn the drill. Your style of selling is developed and honed on the outside waves. Momentum rewards you for a job well done, and your fun meter has moved to high gear.

These outside waves may begin to feel familiar and safe for you, maybe too safe. The problem with safe is the temptation for you to become sloppy, putting your momentum at risk.

Being too comfortable on outside sales waves looks like this:

❖ Selling to your established accounts because you feel the most comfortable there.

❖ Showing up for sales appointments unprepared. Because of your familiarity with these customers, you end up winging it.

❖ Getting sloppy in staying up with your customers' changing needs and finding that your competitor has stolen them away.

We get sloppy mentally and emotionally because we're overconfident; we've handled these waves before. The problem is, we were never designed to stay on these waves! The outside waves are supposed to prepare us, not paralyze us, for the bigger waves to come.

And there are bigger waves to come.

Wave Level 3: Monster Momentum Waves

As the waves get bigger, the amount of risk goes up. But so does the quality of the surfer's ride. *Surfer* magazine says that the bigger the waves, the more exhilarating the experience. The amount of momentum that is pulsing through the water at this level is incredible. Waves of forty to fifty feet high will give any surfer the thrill of his life as he navigates monster waves with total commitment. Here, at this level, the surfer is totally accountable with no room for a sloppy, casual performance. The surfer's ability to ride these waves starts with being in excellent physical condition, reading the waves and knowing when to paddle out. The surfer who hesitates, lacks commitment, or loses focus once he or she picks a wave, can pay dearly.

I had to see these monster waves for myself. So on twenty-four hours' notice I flew out to the Mavericks Surf Contest at Half Moon Bay, near my hometown of San Francisco, California. I had read about these monster waves that every year give surfers the ride of their lives. With friends Brent and Tommy, I stood there, the ground rumbling under our feet, in absolute awe at the sight of the monster waves as they reared their mighty heads to our disbelief and the surfers' delight. These monster waves ranged from forty to fifty feet—it was like a five-story building barreling right toward us! We couldn't believe our eyes. Now I understood how surfing legend Mark Foo could have lost his life surfing these Mavericks waves.

To successfully finish the ride on these astonishing waves, surfers demonstrate the height of self-management. As one surfer bluntly stated, "There are no opinions in big waves. You either make it or you don't!" This surfer is totally accountable and committed to his final results!

What if you had that degree of self-management commitment? What would your sales ride look like? I have some ideas. You would:

❖ Never take a repeat sale for granted.

❖ Work from a strategy and execute.

❖ Know your sales weakness so that your customers don't.

❖ Position yourselves as peers and consultants, not vendors.

❖ Own your day and limit time stealers.

❖ Always manage your new business pipeline.

❖ Constantly look for uncommon ways to serve your established customers—in ways they don't expect.

❖ Build loyalty. Your competitors wouldn't be able to figure out why accounts stay loyal to you, even though you have the higher-priced service or product.

❖ Never blame others for your mistakes. You'd fix it quickly, assume responsibility, and give customers more than they would have received initially.

Any one of these items can become a catalyst for greater events in our sales day. The key idea here is that we must manage them. Waiting for them to happen, assuming they will happen, or wishing they would happen can lead us into some pretty big wipeouts.

When you own your accountability in the sales field, momentum is waiting to reward you. And not surprisingly, at this level the waves aren't quite as crowded.

In an interview on Spike TV, one of surfing's big-wave riders, Laird Hamilton, said that people will fight you for a two-foot wave but they'll give you a twenty-foot wave. "The number of big-wave riders, the ones with true desire will always dwindle down to a courageous few," he explained.

Get off the beach. Be the one.

Michael, like a kid at Christmas, couldn't wait to show me the ocean. So he jumped in my rental car and we headed to my new classroom, the Pacific Ocean. Wow!

We arrived at oceanfront, climbed out of the car, and headed up the steps to the platform overlooking the ocean. With the smell of salt water in the air, the sound of chattering seagulls, and my new friend by my side, we reached the top of the steps that led down to the beach. And like a Rembrandt, before us was God's masterpiece, the mighty Pacific Ocean, staring at us in all its power and glory. Michael was beaming.

I, on the other hand, just wanted to throw up!

If you don't go, you won't know.

3

THE ALLURE
OF SMALL WAVES

Emotions: Friend or Foe?

For the first time, the reality of my decision to surf overwhelmed me like a tsunami wave. The waves were twenty feet tall. Okay, only six feet, but they felt like twenty! Surfers say that waves aren't measured in feet and inches, but in increments of fear. So, in fear measurements the waves were fifty feet tall! My emotions were running high.

I tried to keep my composure on the outside, but on the inside my mind was screaming, "This is too much for me to handle! My kids were right! How can I get out of this?"

My thoughts just kept getting louder until my body followed suit, and my right hand grabbed what I'm sure *felt like a death grip around Michael's muscled forearm. I turned and whimpered, "I can't do this, Michael!" Now shaking with fear, yet a firm determination in my voice, I turned to Michael and said, "Honestly, I appreciate your offering to teach me to surf, but here's a better idea. Let's just go to Plan B. How about if I just watch you guys surf, we'll have a few beers with the guys, and then I can interview you for the book and we'll call it a day." I knew full well, however, Michael wasn't going to buy Plan B!*

The allure of Plan B is so powerful, isn't it? It's not exactly what we set out to do, but it's close. It becomes our safety net when the reality of Plan A starts to sink in and get tough. Here's the real problem: Plan B is never as great. Plan B is never everything we desire, and the rewards are never quite as high. By knowing in the back of our mind that if things don't work out we can always fall back on Plan B, it can so easily become our own "mental prenuptial agreement." At least we get to walk away with something, right? Here's a thought: What if Plan B then becomes a bit of a struggle—hey, we can always go to Plan C. How about Plan D? The problem comes when we let our emotions overwhelm us and steal our commitment to Plan A. It can happen so easily.

Michael's heart is as big as the ocean, but he wasn't buying Plan B. Darn! I was pretty certain trying to sell him on Plan C probably wasn't going to work either. So, like a gentle parent calming his scared child on her first day of kindergarten, Michael gently peeled my white knuckles off of his forearm and squared my shoulders toward him. He smiled empathetically, with a look in his eye that told me he had probably heard the pleadings of Plan B from other overzealous surf protégées. "Eloise Owens, of course fear is high, because knowledge is low. We haven't taught you anything yet," he reassuringly explained.

Instantly my blood pressure stopped soaring and a quietness of thought permeated my screaming brain just long enough for me to reconsider Plan A just one more time. More openly, I headed down the flight of steps to the crystal blue waters ahead. Oddly, the waves no longer seemed as big as they had moments before.

There I stood in my new, very cute flipflops, as the ocean's cold waves splashed over my feet. I gazed out at the horizon. Michael, however, gazed down at my feet. Later, I would come to understand why.

THE ENERGY OF EMOTIONS

As humans, we were created with vibrant emotions. This ability to "feel" is our birthright on this planet; it connects us all. But when we let our emotions rule us, they can ruin us. Unmanaged emotions have cost people relationships, disconnected best friends, and sent our customers straight to our competitors. On the other hand, I have witnessed sales pros using emotions in the best way to achieve great things. So, are emotions our friend or foe? Well, here's the deal—they can be both. On the positive side, emotions are a powerful connector. Given the choice, would you rather have customers who were rationally committed to you in a sales relationship, or emotionally committed to you? Where would greater loyalty rest? I want emotional connections to my clients, don't you? Let the competition try and steal emotionally connected clients away. Fat chance!

But here's the other side to that deal. Emotions can also disrupt us. They can stir us, blind us, disconnect us, and devastate us if we don't know how to manage them. Here are three ways these disruptive emotions can devastate momentum toward our goals.

1. *Disruptive emotions can distort information.*

The waves looked so much more ominous when thoughts evoked by emotional fear were screaming in my head. Oddly though, when I got down to the beach, the waves didn't seem as high. Michael was right: fear is high when knowledge is low. Disruptive emotions have a way of exaggerating the truth in front of us, playing with our resolve and tempting us that Plan B is the smarter way. When more information is added to the mix, emotions become more balanced.

2. *Disruptive emotions can weaken enthusiasm.*

Emotions are contagious. They can have a huge impact on the people around you. People always rise to a person's highest emotions. So in selling, if you want people to be excited about your product or service, you get there first and take them with you. Enthusiasm is a great connector. Your customers and prospects formulate a sense about you pretty quickly.

If they sense you are showing up out of duty, habit, routine, or desperation, they will be less drawn to you. People react more positively to enthusiasm. Let your enthusiasm weaken, and watch out.

3. Disruptive emotions play games with your goals.

Instead of being a person who learns to ride the waves, you *become* a wave—up one minute and down the next. Monday you're on fire, but by Wednesday, well, not so much. By Friday, Plan D is starting to look pretty good, and you go home for the weekend feeling like you've done great things for the week. Hey! Whatever happened to Plan A?

Self-managing emotions is a tough business. Isn't it time for you to get clear about where you are headed in your career and not let disruptive emotions justify smaller

Disruptive emotions are dangerous to momentum.

success? Disruptive emotions are dangerous to momentum. It can keep both surfers and salespeople in the whitewater. But luckily, there are emotions just as powerful that spark momentum. I call them the 3-Ds. They are *desire*, *drive*, and *determination*.

THE POWER OF THE 3-D'S

Give me a salesperson with desire, drive, and determination any day, and I will show you a momentum champion in the making. At the heart of all elite athletes is the desire to be great, coupled with a drive and determination that make them unstoppable. Momentum loves this trio of forces! Let's take a closer look at these three momentum drivers.

Desire

Desire is a powerful feeling. It is highly emotional. *Webster's* defines *desire* as "to want something very strongly; a wish, craving, or longing for something." Retailers have done research that indicates that when people are shown products that they desire, they actually feel something physically. A smart retailer knows they are in the business of creating desire within their customers. If they can create a strong enough desire, the customer will move heaven and earth to buy.

Everyone has desires. That is how we are wired. But we don't all desire the same things. My son, for example, can't stop reading books. He craves reading anything he can get his hands on. For his birthday one year I took him to Half Price Books in Dallas. You should have seen his face light up! He could have stayed there all day. I, on the other hand, well, give me tickets to a Cowboys game, and now we're talkin'. I had no desire to stare at racks of used books all day, but the reason I stayed in that bookstore was because I have a strong desire—and great delight—in making my son's face light up. Same destination, different desires.

For desire to be the most effective in your sales goals, it must be defined with great clarity—absolute clarity—your clarity. What about you? What do you desire? How clear are your desires connected to your goals? Can you feel them? What do you see?

Most salespeople suffer from fuzzy pictures. That can happen when you allow others to create your pictures for you. When this happens, your desires will be mediocre at best. Moving in a direction set for you by someone else—using their budgets and quotas—can be limiting and lifeless. Clear up the pictures. Make them yours. Make them emotionally your own.

Drive

Desire alone is useless unless it moves us to decision. Many salespeople can describe their goals in great detail. Now what? That's where drive, the second *D*, comes into play. To paraphrase Aristotle, "Drive

Desire alone is useless unless it moves us to decision.

always moves through desire." You could say that desire is the catalyst for our drive to wake up and start getting serious about doing something. It's our decision engine. *Webster's* states that our drive is the part of the mind that consciously decides things; it's where the power to make decisions comes from.

Determination

The third *D*, determination, establishes our course of action with firmness of purpose or intent. The key here is that our course of action is intertwined with our desire and drive. How many times have we planned a course of action in any undertaking only to abandon it weeks later? How about diets, goal setting, or quitting smoking?

The more determination you have to act on your decision, borne out of your desires, the easier momentum is to build and sustain. So, desire is the spark; drive is putting that spark into motion; and determination keeps us on track. Out of your desire, drive, and determination comes a commitment that conquers distraction and moves you powerfully toward your goals.

Self-managing emotions is not for the faint-hearted. Disruptive emotions are powerful. They can kill your 3-Ds faster than anything! The following story demonstrates just how powerful these disruptive emotions can be.

THE LEGEND OF LONG LEGS

It was January 1, 1981. I sat up in bed with a new kind of determination, seeing a vision of sorts for my new sales year ahead. Maybe I was just tired of seeing other sales reps walk across the stage every year showered with accolades. I decided, this year it was my turn to take that walk. I wanted to be the National Sales Award winner this year and found the very thought of it tremendously exhilarating and highly emotional.

I used New Year's Day in 1981 to plan my attack to achieving my goals. The energy from my excitement kept me focused and determined as I strategized how to keep sales high all year long. I visualized my acceptance speech on stage in front of hundreds of sales colleagues. It was all so clear.

What I soon discovered, however, was that there was another sales rep a thousand miles away in Bloomington, Indiana, who woke up with the exact same vision! She was just as emotionally committed to being number one. And what made matters worse, she was new to the company. I hate new people. You know, the really enthusiastic, positive people who are always cheerful because they don't know any better. She was highlighted in our company newsletter as the up-and-coming new talent. "Yeah, right," I muttered to myself, tossing the newsletter in the garbage can where it belonged. This was my year. No new girl on the block was going to steal my goal away! This meant war!

As the first-quarter revenue numbers were posted, I breathed a sigh of satisfaction, noting that I was comfortably

No new girl on the block was going to steal my goal away! This meant war!

in first place. My eyes then scanned down the list, and, sure enough, there was that new girl from Bloomington, Indiana, gaining ground. She broke into the top ten national sales ranks. I didn't like what I saw.

Heading into our second quarter, I received an envelope in the mail from the company. I was so focused that I forgot all about the upcoming summer leadership retreat. It was an open invitation to all top ten national sales reps to meet together in Park City, Utah, for a weekend of networking and strategizing. I scanned the list of the invitees, and my knees went weak. You guessed it. The new little hotshot sales rep had made the list. A new strategy was about to be born. Everyone else could go to this retreat to network and strategize. Not me. I was going for one reason—to meet the enemy face to face. It started to feel like the Rumble in the Jungle—Muhammad Ali meeting George Foreman as they met face to face for the prebout weigh-in. I couldn't wait.

The weekend finally arrived, and we old-timers eagerly greeted each other in the beautiful conference center nestled in the stunning mountain setting. There was no sign of the new girl. "Typical. She'll probably come in late to make her grand entrance," I muttered. I knew her type—the flash in the pan. Have you ever decided you didn't like someone, even before you've met them? Me, too. Now was that time, and I was feeling anxious.

Finally, with minutes left before our retreat was to begin, the door swung open and in walked a woman with a very familiar face. I recognized her from the company newsletter—and my office dartboard! Being the more mature of the two, I made the first move, immediately racing over to her, extending my hand to shake hers. "Hi. My name is Eloise Owens," I confidently touted.

She responded back with equal confidence. "Oh yes. I know who you are." Smugly I thought, *Yeah, good answer, new girl.* She was tall with long flowing brown hair, big brown eyes, and boy, was she thin. Now, I really hated her. I nicknamed her on the spot—Long Legs. She called me Owens.

We sat down together, side by side. What's the old saying—keep your friends close and your enemies closer? She was never out of my sight. We were inseparable all weekend. Soon I discovered, to my dismay, that this new girl was actually pretty cool. She was funny and smart with a Midwestern charm that was very endearing. Before I knew it, we were becoming fast friends.

The weekend flew by, and as we both caught the shuttle-bus back to the airport, we hugged each other good-bye at the curb. As I turned to grab my luggage and head to my gate, I felt an arm reach out and clamp down hard on my left forearm with a voice that shook me to the core. It was Long Legs, transformed from Princess Charming into Satan herself. With a fire in her eyes that shot right through me, she said, "Hey, Owens, by the way, I hope you *like* second place!"

Speechless and stunned, I watched her confidently walk away. Now boarding the airplane home, I was a lot less confident than when I arrived. I needed some time to regroup.

What Long Legs didn't realize, though, was knowing whom she was messing with. My dad was a U.S. Marine, and his youngest of four girls was not going to let some verbal scare tactics take her off course. Instead, I returned home determined more than ever to outwit, outplay, and outlast Long Legs. My fourth quarter, as a result, was absolutely unbelievable. I knew that when December 31 finally arrived, my buddy Long Legs would be sent packing. This tribe had spoken!

What a year! I was tired, but it was a good tired. Now, all I had to do was wait for our annual sales conference in January when the winner for the 1981 National Sales Award would be announced. I slept very well.

What was the difference between this year and so many others? I don't believe it was merely one thing; it was actually three emotional elements that elevated my sales game to a different level for unthinkable results. It was the power of the 3-Ds: desire, drive, and determination. Boy, if I could just bottle and sell these three ingredients!

Finally, the day I had dreamed about for a whole year had arrived. All the sales leaders met in Salt Lake City for a preconference workshop, and this time Long Legs raced to find me. She gave me a big hug and told me she'd heard I'd had a monster fourth quarter. I was grinning from ear to ear. She then said the words I dreamed of hearing, "Congratulations, Owens, on your win. It has been quite a year!"

When hard work pays off and you see the fruits of your labor, it puts you on top of the world.

Wow! Achieving your goals is such a great feeling. When hard work pays off and you see the fruits of your labor, it puts you on top of the world. Now it had finally arrived—Saturday night—the night when they would announce the winner and the celebration would begin. It was bigger and better than I imagined. Boy, I love selling.

Awards Night

Gazing around the Majestic Ballroom of the Marriott Hotel in Salt Lake City with six hundred other sales colleagues was almost more than I could stand. I was so excited. My stomach had butterflies as I pushed my food around the plate, pretending to be enjoying the dinner. Out of the corner of my eye I noticed across the ballroom that someone stood up. It was Long Legs. *Where is she going,* I wondered. We were close to starting the award ceremony as the audiovisual team finished their last microphone checks. The president was taking the stage.

With urgency in her step, Long Legs was weaving in between the round tables looking for someone—me. Our eyes locked and she motioned me over to her side of the room. *What does she want?* With an irritated look on my face, I thought her timing couldn't be worse. We were getting ready to start. Jumping up from my chair, I quickly wove my way through the tables to meet her. I noticed she had something in her hands.

As I approached her, she smiled broadly and warmly and said, "I know we are getting ready to start, but I wanted to give you this gift before we went up on stage." I never even thought to get her a gift. On top of being excited and nervous, great—now I'm feeling guilty, too. She handed me the gift and explained quickly, "My husband travels internationally and he brought this back from Indonesia. I wanted you to have it." In her hands was draped this exquisite silk scarf. It was so beautiful, filled with rich colors in a tapestry pattern fit for a queen. It felt soft as a feather in my opened hands. Overwhelmed at this most unexpected gift, I reached out and hugged Long Legs just as the president leaned into the microphone and announced for all the top ten finalists to now take the stage. Turning to bolt back to my chair to drop off the scarf, I immediately felt a familiar death grip on my right forearm! Satan was back! I turned toward Long Legs

I turned toward Long Legs to see that fire back in her eyes as she spewed out her words with venom. to see that fire back in her eyes as she spewed out her words with venom. "Hey, Owens, in Indonesia they call that a crying towel. I thought you just might need it tonight!"

Whaaat? I was convinced this girl had lost her mind. I've heard of being a sore loser before, but come on now. Get a grip, new girl! I broke free from her grasp to hurriedly drop the scarf on the back of my chair as we both took the stage—on opposite ends.

I tried to visualize what this night would be like, but

my visions were not big enough for reality. It was even more exhilarating, more exciting than I could ever have imagined. The air was electric. Chandeliers that glistened like diamonds illuminated the ballroom. Six hundred sales professionals, dressed to the nines, became a sea of smiling faces, each cheering loudly as we stepped on the stage.

The president welcomed all to the evening—the countdown to number one had begun! One by one he announced the names. "Number ten, nine, eight, seven . . . We all scooted in as my sales colleagues from around the nation received their awards to the applause of hundreds and exited stage right. Politely clapping for all of them, I still had my eye on Long Legs. The president continued, "Number six, five, four." By now the crowd was screaming at a high pitch as three more exited stage right. He continued and called out number three. It was a friend of mine from the West Coast. I leaned in to hug him as he, too, exited stage right. Finally, there were only two left standing, Owens and Long Legs! Like two boxers in the ring, fighting it out all year long, it was now our time!

What a night! A hush fell over the crowd as the president motioned for the crowd to quiet down. "Before I announce the winner," he explained to the anxious crowd, "I want to let all of you know that the difference that separates these two top performers is $74.36." The crowd gasped! My stomach tightened. Then the president, glancing down at his list to double check, leaned in, pressed his lips against the podium microphone and proclaimed, "The 1981 National Sales Award Winner *Runner Up*, from Dallas, Texas . . . Eloise Owens!" Nooooo! My heart exploded! I swallowed hard, fighting back overwhelming emotions as I stepped forward to receive my second place plaque and considerably lower bonus check. I was escorted to stage right where I would now painfully listen to Long Legs' acceptance speech. Quickly glancing out in the crowd, I could see my empty seat—the scarf draped over the back of my chair, an all too vivid reminder of Long Legs' final words.

I was about to learn a very emotional $74.36 lesson.

W-I-P-E-O-U-T

4

WILL YOU SURF
OR GO HOME?

Managing Expectations in Your Sales World

One minute you're a bronze god, cheating fate, sliding free, then you're flipped into the drink—your arms sprawled, eyes bugged, lungs burning, completely at the mercy of the wave—helpless. Wipeouts take proud postures and make them look silly."

—The Unridden Realm

What's the most fragile thing you own? For me it would have to be a beautiful, signed Lladro sculpture of a man and woman dancing elegantly in a circle. It sits majestically in my lighted curio cabinet in my home.

When my kids were little, they would love to play wrestle

mania in the living room near the cabinet where stood my pride and joy, the Lladro sculpture. I remember more than once yelling into the living room during one of their bouts, "Be careful! Remember the Lladro!" (Sounds a lot like "Remember the Alamo!") My kids have kidded me over the years that if there were ever a house fire, they would be on their own to get out because Mom's going for the Lladro first! It is so fragile that I always felt the need to give it extra attention, to protect it and guard it from any possible damage.

FRAGILE THINGS

As a salesperson, have you ever wondered what is your most fragile possession? Ever thought about what you should be protecting? I never really thought about it before.

> **Crash! I can still hear my desire, drive, and determination crashing to the floor like a shattered Lladro sculpture.**

If I told you it was your desire, drive, and determination, would you believe me? See, the real story of Long Legs is not what happened in the twelve months in 1981, but what happened for the first six months of 1982. I fell out of the top ten nationally for the first time in my lengthy career with that company. My sales performance dropped to some of my worst sales totals since I began working for the company. I lost more than an award for 1981. I totally lost my momentum, and my results showed it!

Crash! I can still hear my desire, drive, and determination crashing to the floor like a shattered Lladro sculpture. Can't you? When things don't exactly go the way we expect, it affects us emotionally. And when emotions are stirred, watch out! Our 3-Ds will be the first place to take the hit! Haven't some of our worst decisions come as a result of letting our emotions overwhelm our actions? I was becoming the poster child!

You don't have to lose a national sales award to know what that feels like. Faces I have met over ten years as a sales coach flash in my mind—great salespeople who forgot to protect their drive and determination to be great, who chose instead to settle for smaller waves. Salespeople with all the ability in the world, yet have mediocre drive, desire, and determination. Sometimes, self-management of the 3-Ds takes a backseat to disruptive emotions. These disruptive emotions are dangerous; they're momentum killers. They are *missed expectations, disappointment,* and *regret.* Any one of these can send us reeling emotionally, but when all three hit, well, it can feel like a tsunami wave.

MISSED EXPECTATIONS,
DISAPPOINTMENT, AND REGRET

Have you ever considered where your expectations come from? In your mind, they seemed perfectly reasonable. The problems come when expectations are in your head and the other party is clueless.

Missed expectations can defeat the most committed salespeople. It can reduce their will, desire, and determination to a whimper, sending them straight into the whitewater, drowning in lower momentum. It can happen to the very best of us when we least expect it! It happened to me. I didn't expect to lose to Long Legs that night.

Now, fast-forward to some twenty years later. I wasn't expecting what happened next on my surf adventure either. Get ready.

As I approached the Willis brothers' surf headquarters, I immediately observed that it was noticeably quiet. There was no one in sight. I found that odd. Hmmm, I looked at my watch again, 9:59 a.m. The student had arrived, so where was the teacher? I continued through the garage and headed toward the backyard. Suddenly

Milton peaked his head out from among the surfboards leaning up against the outside wall of the garage.

Curious, I asked, "Where's Michael?" His response was not what I expected.

"Oh, Michael has surf lessons all day today. He has been in the water since 7:00 a.m."

Looking puzzled, I repeated back to Milton, Michael's words to me just twelve hours before: "Meet me in the garage at 10:00 a.m." The student had arrived but the teacher was a no-show.

Just then, a beautiful Japanese woman named Sanami walked up the driveway and greeted Milton. She was Milton's next student ready to hit the waves. He welcomed her and introduced me. He then told her he was ready, so they headed down the driveway. As they left, he yelled back to me, "Have a great day, Eloise Owens. We'll see you down at the beach." They then disappeared down the driveway!

Just like a monster wave crashing over me, I began to get, well, just a little irritated! Okay, a lot irritated! I kept thinking, is this how they treat all their guests?

I picked up my cell phone and called one of my brainy friends, Gary, who had made it clear that he thought I should never have gone on this stupid trip in the first place. I needed some advice. Thinking I had already surfed, Gary answered, "Is this surfer girl?" to which I snapped, "No, it's "left-standing-in-the-garage-girl!" I explained rather loudly how I had been stood up and left all by myself. "Can you believe it?" I fumed.

Gary immediately checked flights back to Dallas as we tried to figure out what to do next. I was conflicted. I wanted to go home, but I wasn't ready to give up just yet. So I told my friend to give me some time to think. We agreed to talk in a few hours. He continued to check the flights back to Big D while I continued to just get mad! I walked back down the driveway and got into my rental car and slammed the door!

About an hour later my cell phone rang and it was my friend Christine. She had already heard from Gary on the latest turn of events.

"Eloise, I don't think you are there by accident," she said.

*"I believe you are there for a reason, and if you leave now,
you may never know why you made this connection in the
first place." I love my friend Christine, but at that moment
I hated her advice. I knew that despite all of the emotions
I was feeling, she was speaking truth. I just didn't want to
hear it!*

Think about a time when what you got from someone important was nothing even close to what you expected. Be ready for the emotions to stir. Underneath the emotion of the situation lies the true culprit, a clash of expectations. Would you expect any missed expectations between two surfer dudes and a corporate saleswoman?!

**Underneath the
emotion of the
situation lies
the true
culprit, a clash
of expectations.**

The World of the Saleswoman

She's a saleswoman and a frequent flyer who lives a life pretty much dominated by time. She owns a variety of wristwatches that she always wears and would rather die than leave home not knowing what time it is. She is never late for her appointments; she was taught that if you're not ten minutes early for an appointment, you're late! She takes great pride in ending all speeches on time (a mark of a true professional) and believes strongly in being on time because of the respect it shows for the other person. Did I mention her dad was a Marine? She seems to have a knack for multitasking, making the most use of her time by doing three things at once. She can talk on the cell phone and put on her makeup while driving with her knee. Hey, she's a salesperson, all right!

The World of a Surfer

First off, most surfers don't own a wristwatch. They are dudes who just, well, experience time. Every day brings new things if you just open yourself up and go with the flow. Their day consists of an early morning coffee to get a sense of what the day will bring. They check the weather reports, surf reports, and feel the early morning wind on their face to see how clear the waves will be that day. Every day is perfect. You just adapt to what each day gives you, being thankful for it all. The most important thing in your day is to remember to breeeeathe. If you just slow down enough in your day, you will see things around you that you might have never, ever noticed before. By slowing down with the people around you, you will be more present with them. These surfers do one thing at a time. They eat when the time is right. No set time, no set place. Everything always works out perfectly.

Driving around for hours along Highway 101 was not what I expected to be doing my first full day in sunny Southern California. There were enough beaches along the shoreline to keep me busy hunting for my surf instructor for an entire week! By three o'clock, with no sign of any surfers that I recognized, I threw in the beach towel and decided to head back to Dana's house, where I was staying. Being tired from all the emotions swirling, I just wanted to take a nap. I needed to rest and think.

No wonder I was so tired. I had stepped into what felt like was another world. A land of different expectations that was not even close to mine. Not even close! The worlds of the saleswoman and the surfer are so far apart. This is also true, sometimes just as dramatically, with salespeople and their managers.

DIFFERENT SALES WORLDS

Talk about different expectations, have you ever wondered what planet your manager stepped off of? Whew! I have,

Talk about different expectations, have you ever wondered what planet your manager stepped off of?

many times, in my younger sales days. And managers, how about your sales team? Aliens, huh? We expect certain things from people all around us every day. The problems begin when we assume that our expectations are universal.

Looking at the table on the following page, it's no wonder salespeople and sales managers are frustrated with each other. When expectations are missed, it can so easily move us into the second phase: the disappointment. Talk about emotional! Whew! Now your emotions flare, your body feels the stress, big time, and your desire, drive, and determination leak out like air from a blown tire! Many people have reported that at this phase they actually feel a heaviness throughout their body.

Salespeople's Expectations	Sales Manager's Expectations
Managers are here to fix our problems. I expect answers.	Good salespeople are good problem solvers. Don't bring me the problems. I expect to hear solutions from my salespeople. That shows me initiative.
I deserve the exception to a company policy because I work hard for the company.	If I give out this one exception to the company's policy, I will open up a Pandora's box for the next time. I expect salespeople to suck it up and play by the rules. After all, rules are rules.
If I produce high results, I will be promoted and/or given a raise.	I expect salespeople in our company to see the big picture. Just because they had a good year doesn't mean our whole department did. This is a team effort here!
I expect my manager to be available for me when I need him or her.	I expect my team members to manage their time and not keep interrupting my day. Don't they see how busy and important I am?
My company should provide the tools for me to do my job; that is, laptops, collateral materials on time, etc. I should not have to buy a thing.	Salespeople should invest in themselves if they want to be successful. I never had a laptop when I was a sales rep.
Every company should provide additional perks for its employees.	We pay our people a very competitive wage. They should be thankful they have a job with benefits.
As a top performer, I expect to be recognized for my efforts.	We always put our top producers in the company newsletter. Gee, what more do they expect?

I woke up an hour later. It was now 5:00 p.m. My cell phone showed missed calls, probably from Gary letting me know the evening flights I could catch back to Dallas. Being tempted to call my friend back, I decided to try Michael's number first to see if anyone was back from the beach yet. I dialed his number.

He must have seen from caller ID that it was me, because the first words out of his mouth when he answered made me want to jump through the phone line and choke him!

"Eloise Owens, where were you today? He said in a loud, irritated tone. You missed a great day of surfing. We even saw dolphins!"

In a louder tone, I answered his question, "Michael, I was exactly where you told me to be — in the garage at 10:00 a.m. Where were you?" I was honestly hoping for a good explanation so I could move past the pain of disappointment. Did these guys have any idea how much they had let me down? I had been looking forward to this trip for a long time. All my clients, friends, and family were expecting to hear from this new surfer girl.

Judging from Michael's response, I was guessing not. In fact, his answer only made it worse. He didn't really have a good answer except that he was busy teaching others to surf and was expecting me to join him at the 15th Street beach, and he would work me in when he could. *Where in the heck is 15th Street?* I wondered silently. The silence, however, didn't last for long.

With both barrels, I let him have it! "Michael, how in the heck was I supposed to find you when I have never been there before? Did you even stop and wonder that maybe you forgot to give me all the information?"

He got louder, too, and snapped, "What exactly do you want from me?"

The rest of the call just got louder, each of us trying to justify our own expectations. Michael expected me to go with the flow and show up. I expected to be treated like a guest and that Michael would make me feel welcome and safe. Neither happened. That was the conversation on the surface. But like most disconnects, sooner or later, the real reasons start to surface. And up they popped!

After a brief silence in the conversation (I think we were both reloading), Michael said he and Milton both thought I wasn't ready for the experience.

"Whaaaaat?" I yelled.

Michael explained his reasoning. "When I walked with you down to the water the day before, you walked in the ocean with your shoes [flipflops] on. That told me that you weren't ready to surf. To become a surfer you must embrace the ocean and get connected to it. You can only do that with your feet in the water." I was speechless! How was I supposed to know this?

Well, this was Michael's expectation, which was born out of living in Hawaii for twenty years. In the book Walking on Water, author Andy Martin recounts receiving the shoe lecture from Michael. Michael told Andy, "If you wear shoes, you're not grounded. You're out of touch with the earth. It's like riding around in a car and never getting out. You might as well be on Mars.'"[1]

Andy commented after being shoeless for the rest of the day that he could feel the long grass beneath his feet with a sensual awareness he had never experienced before. Walking, or just standing still, had become a pleasure. Michael was right. Unfortunately, I was not privy to this information while arguing with Michael on the phone. In my anger, it never dawned on me to try and understand his thinking and expectations.

Are there people who you disagree with, who frustrate you to no end? Have you ever stopped to wonder about the reason for their point of view?

I had always taken great pride in the fact that I was a great debater (actually, a great arguer). I could hold my own with the best of them. Politics, religion, you name it, Eloise would jump right in. But wearing flipflops in the ocean? I knew I was in over my head! All I could do was breathe, trying to conjure up what little patience I had left to see if there was anything here left to salvage.

At this moment only one thing was perfectly clear to me: I had no desire, drive, or determination left to surf! Period! So I offered one last idea up to Michael, with no real confidence that he would go for it. It was my Plan Z. I figured I had nothing left to lose.

So I said, "Well, obviously, this wasn't supposed to be my surfing debut, but that's okay. I'm still going to write this book, even if I never surf. So, Michael, what would you think about us meeting tomorrow and let me ask you some questions about surfing—maybe get a few quotes for the book—and we'll say our good-byes?"

What's the worst he could say? Well, I got the worst he could say with both barrels. Michael quickly gave me a response I was not ready for: "Eloise Owens, how can you so easily lie to yourself? You know if you got on that *airplane to go home without surfing, you would regret it for the rest of your life! This trip was not for some quick sound bites for a book, and you know it."*

Ouch! I was busted! Michael had sensed my cop-out plan and had the guts to call me on it. I sat in silence. Knowing in my heart that this surfer saw right through me, I conceded, in a much quieter voice, that maybe he was right. I would regret going home and not learning to surf, but at this particular moment, it just felt too hard to commit to trying it again.

Ever been there? The emotions of the moment are so high, just the thought of redirecting any energy toward action is almost nauseating. Walking away seems like the best alternative when there is no desire to try again. The disruptive emotions have won. But are we totally at their mercy? What if we learned to step back and look at them instead of letting them rule us? Looking at the root of the emotions can provide great insight.

What happened to this surfer girl's will to defy what some

family and friends said was a crazy idea in the first place? What happened to all that desire, drive, and determination that got me to California in the first place? It was as if my 3-Ds fell like dominoes, one hitting the other, from missed expectations to deep disappointment, to now the rein of regret. This perfect storm had hit this surfer girl's wannabe, now not wanting very much anymore. It felt like 1982 with Long Legs all over again!

STAY AND SURF OR GO HOME?

What would you do? I have asked audiences across the country: Would you stay and surf or go home? The answers range anywhere from "Stay and surf" to "I'd be on the next flight home" to one man in New Jersey whose response made me smile: "I would never have gone in the first place because it's not that important to me!"

Here's the point. It always comes back to the question, How badly do you want it? What is your desire level? You have to answer that question first, because that answer will determine how unstoppable you will be in getting what you want. I was ready to go home because I let failed expectations grab my emotions, pull me down, and kill my desire.

I did the next best thing and gave Michael a "maybe."
My promise to him as we hung up was that I would be
in the garage the next day at 10:00 a.m., either to surf
or to say good-bye. "I will see you in the garage at 10:00
a.m. tomorrow to hear your decision," he responded.
"Good night, Eloise Owens."

At that point, I didn't know whether my desire, drive, and
determination could outweigh the disruptive emotions of
missed expectations, disappointment, and regret of my trip.

How about you? When things don't go your way, when
expectations are crossed, will you surf, or go home?

Michael Willis shares his passion for surfing with eager students.

5

FACING MONSTER
WAVES

Building a Momentum Mindset

The next morning, I packed for the airport. I was tired,
confused, and drained of energy. The only plan I could
come up with was to meet the brothers in the garage at
10:00 a.m. to say good-bye. I felt defeated. I was not
looking forward to our final meeting. In fact, I dreaded
it. I hugged Michael and Milton's sister good-bye as I
left the house where I stayed and began the thirty-minute
drive to surfer headquarters, the garage. The closer I got,
the worse I felt, in a sweaty-palms sort of way.

As I silently drove through the canyons, I wished
again for that voice . . . you know . . . the Moses-on-the-
mountain voice. Again, I didn't hear from Moses, but I

did hear from Julie! Not in a verbal sense, but from the recollection of a picture she drew me years ago while I sat in her black leather ergodynamic chair as she listened to me wallowing in the whitewater. The picture from that day instantly flashed before my eyes as I continued to travel the winding canyon road.

As I drove to WB Surfing headquarters, I heard that familiar and trusted "voice" of my former district manager, Julie. She and I had formed a bond through the years, working together for a national seminar company. But she saw weakness in this salesperson who was frustrated with the monster waves ahead of her. Although I'd been presented with an opportunity to reach for higher sales goals, Julie only heard why the goal she presented to me was unreasonable and my three very thought-out demands she would have to meet in order for me to accept the challenge.

Now I'm cringing again, just thinking of Julie calling my bluff. She wasn't bothered by my tantrum. She just patiently took out a single sheet of blank paper and drew this model:

C > E

This is a simple concept, but it's one that had a significant career-changing impact on my life. Here's what she gently began to teach.

The C stands for *cause*, and the E stands for *effect*. Or more simply, she said, "Cause is always greater than effect."

My furrowed brow showed her I was confused. I wasn't sure where she was going. Julie asked me to erase in my mind the usual definitions of cause and effect while she handed me a pen along with her drawing. Next she asked me to write this question under the Cause side of the equation: "What will you *cause* to happen today?" Then she looked up and smiled. I wasn't smiling. Remaining undaunted by my look of confusion, she then asked me to write another question under the Effect side of this equation: "What will you allow to hinder your effectiveness today? What she was really asking is, What excuses are you hanging on to? She then began to explain that it is most natural for us mentally to gravitate toward the Effect side of the equation when first

What will you CAUSE to happen today?

faced with a goal. It's easier to let our minds steep in all the reasons why we can't achieve our goals, which hinders our effectiveness and breeds excuses, than it is to fight all the negative voices in our heads and spend our energy on how to cause our goals to happen.

The Effect side of the concept is where we are the most vulnerable mentally because that's where fear loves to play. I had the Effect side of the equation down to an art form. I knew every excuse there was. Thankfully, Julie knew fear when she heard it.

THE THREE FACES OF FEAR

Fear can be useful when it protects and redirects us. Instilled in my kids at a young age, fear served them well to stay away from fire, lawnmowers, and interrupting Mom during a Cowboys football game.

Yet fear can be slavery when it terrorizes and paralyzes us. It is powerful and gains a negative sort of momentum in

Fear first drives us to find "why we can't," then it relieves us of accountability to figure out "how we can."

our brains. Fear first drives us to find "why we can't," then it relieves us of accountability to figure out "how we can." It can make us spectators, watching everybody else succeed in reaching their goals while we are left standing on the beach, justifying why our toes feel so good buried in the warm sand. Perpetual fear can keep us from growing to our next level professionally because it limits the conversations of opportunity in our head. The quiet conversations we have with ourselves either build energy toward our goals on the Cause side of the equation, or destroys energy on the Effect side of the equation, creating a mind filled with excuses.

Fear can also exhaust us. My friend Kevin shared with me the story of how an innocent father-son moment at the ocean off the coast of Florida quickly turned to a moment of terror.

Kevin and his son saw the red warning flag posted at the lifeguard's stand but jumped in the ocean anyway. After all, they were both good swimmers. The red flag alerts swimmers to stay out of the water due to strong riptides, or more accurately, rip currents, in the area.

Suddenly Kevin and his son's best swimming were getting them nowhere. They were being pulled farther and farther away from the shore, and Kevin kept hearing his son cry out, "Dad, I'm so tired!" Trying to hold him up while fighting his own exhaustion, Kevin recognized that they were in deep trouble. Finally someone saw them from the shore and dispatched a rescue team to pull them to safety. When Kevin was safe on the beach, he dropped to the sand in sheer exhaustion.

Watching Kevin as he told me this story, I couldn't get over the expression on his face as he relived the incident and the fact that he used the word *tired* more than seven times. Theirs was a narrow escape as Kevin related that the next day reports came in that two people on the next beach over were not so lucky. The rip currents had won.

Mentally, we have rip currents too. And they can be just as exhausting as fighting Mother Nature. Here are three rip currents, or fears, that can exhaust sales professionals, weakening mindset to gravitate toward excuses and pulling you further away from higher sales results.

1. Fear of Disappointing People

Salespeople can be especially susceptible to the "approval of people" rip currents, which pulls us under in our exhausting attempt to please everyone around us. Being preoccupied with acceptance and approval can be so exhausting. One of my favorite authors, Brennan Manning, writes:

> Because of our suffocating need to please others, we cannot say no with the same confidence in which we say yes. And we are so over extended in people, projects, and causes, motivated not by personal commitment but by the fear of not living up to others' expectations.[1]

How much mental energy are you spending on being accepted and approved by everybody? It can pull you under and keep you mentally exhausted.

Surfers are just so darn cool. But believe it or not, there are those in life who look at their lifestyle with great disdain. They are slackers, undisciplined, and need to get a real job. Here's the funny part. Surfers know people think that about them and *they don't care.* They aren't about to give up their passion for surfing and ocean lifestyle because someone might not approve of their professional choices—or their calling. Michael and Milton Willis have many things they would like to *cause* in their lifetime. Making sure you approve of them is not even close to making their list. But bringing surfing to disadvantaged kids is high on their list. Instilling the surf experience of team building to corporate leaders is on their list. Teaching young kids how to cherish and protect the environment is a major passion. And creating a foundation to perpetuate the spirit of surfing is their cause. Simple focus— no rip currents!

2. Fear of the Unknown

What keeps us on the Effect side of the equation is demanding to operate solely in what is known. We know our customers, our territory, our product line, and we sure as heck know ourselves. Our minds fixate on autopilot "knowns" because the fear of not knowing can so easily trigger our imaginations.

I am convinced big-wave rider Milton Willis would probably be dead today if he let his mind and imagination have free rein as he paddled out to catch those eighty-foot monster waves.

While driving with Milton back from a beautiful, sunny, summer day at the ocean, my curiosity got the best of me. Not knowing for sure if he would answer, I threw this question at him. "Milton, what was it like paddling into an eighty-foot wave when you knew that just one wrong move might kill you instantly?"

"Essential requirement for a big-wave rider is not courage, daring, or fitness but a non-arousable imagination."

His answer in typical Milton style was so simple yet incredibly precise. He turned to me and in a matter-of-fact tone said, "The bigger the wave, the quieter you get."

Another big-wave rider said it this way: "Essential requirement for a big-wave rider is not courage, daring, or fitness but a non-arousable imagination."

If big-wave riders let their minds run wild, they would be rehearsing every death-by-drowning scenario their minds could conjure up. But they don't. To execute at the highest levels in this sport demands mental strength to stay quiet while executing through the unknown. This same skill set, the ability to keep your imagination under control, is just as critical when it comes to your sales career. Take it from a guy named Steve.

Steve was having a great year selling advertising. Over a beer one night, some of his sales colleagues warned him that if he kept up these high numbers, he would have to go up against his own high sales numbers the next year, making it impossible to hit his bonuses. Their talk ignited Steve's imagination with the unknown by painting a picture of financial disaster that would certainly come to him next year. Steve was being seduced by the fear of the unknown. He bought into the fear and it broke his momentum.

Our endless fascination with assuming the worst and

letting our minds have free rein to create our death-by-drowning scenarios give fear so much power over our performance and where we spend our energy. Don't get caught in the "unknown" rip currents. It can wear you out and drown you in doubt.

3. Fear of Familiar Failures

Failures are emotional and mind crippling. They can stay with us a lifetime and drag us under if we aren't mentally tough.

Let's take our past failures, for example. We all have them. But have we ever stopped to consider the powerful influence they still have? Come into my world for a minute. One year, I spoke to a men's group of engineers at their annual conference. This "momentum" lady walks out and dives into her regular shtick and within about ten minutes, I could tell I was in deep trouble. They were just not responding to this girl—at all. Needless to say, as a speaker who takes great pride in the ability to connect with her audiences, it was a painful hour with the boys. I flew home from the conference feeling awful and did my best to put the experience out of my mind. A few months went by and I received another speaking opportunity from a men's group. Before the meeting planner finished explaining the opportunity, I stopped her with a loud, "No thanks!"

I reacted emotionally because of past failure and denied myself a potentially great opportunity.

How many opportunities do we miss because, without thinking, we react according to our past failures? If we allow ourselves to, we can become emotionally hijacked by our own memories and succumb to the mercy of our past.

Instead of emotionally reacting, try to mentally cause a different conversation in your head. Marilyn Brennan, a colleague of mine, introduced me to the three *R*s, as a way to deal with the past: *reflect, reconsider,* and *reframe.* Stop thinking and deciding things based on your past failures. Rather, spend the mental energy to reflect on the situation, rationally reconsider missed data, then reframe the situation to act more powerfully in the present and future.

Applying the three *R*s to my pain of failing in front of the engineers, I would have reflected on that event and reconsidered what I could have done differently to get the result I wanted. For example: I could have done my audience homework, connected with some key audience members before the event to understand their world, and respected the audience enough to throw out my normal shtick and instead bring them what they needed. The reframe showed me that the past failure with the engineers was a gift that would develop my speaking career and enhance future presentations. Mental toughness to focus on learning from the failure would have moved me right back to the Cause side of our equation.

STAYING ON THE CAUSE SIDE OF THE EQUATION

What drives some surfers to surf impossible waves?

Milton Willis says, "Surfing Pipeline [the thriller wave on Hawaii's North Shore] requires much more than technique or bravado. It requires steadfast commitment to catch a wave, stay on the surfboard, and finish the ride. Full-hearted, unwavering commitment is how good surfers become great!"[2]

Surfers can't perform at high levels without commitment and neither can salespeople. What about you? Is your commitment level high or low? Is it full-hearted and unwavering or is it momentary and short-lived?

Extreme Commitment

Are you as committed to reaching your goals as surfers who risk their life on monster waves? Champion surfers don't set a bar of how much they are willing to do before it becomes too much. Their commitment knows no boundaries. They just do whatever it takes. That may include physical conditioning, pioneering new surfboard equipment, or developing better ways to detect oncoming swells.

Funny, but a lot of salespeople never do that. We seem to have a bar set in our brain for reasons of comfort, even fear, so that when we approach the bar and are being asked to do more, we don't have the commitment to do what it takes. Making extra calls, staying late, and coming in early seem like an intrusion in our day—classic symptoms of low commitment. Contrast that with surfer Bethany Hamilton.

On Halloween 2003, Bethany Hamilton was attacked by a fourteen-foot shark while surfing and lost her left arm. By Thanksgiving, this committed teenager-turned-instant-celebrity was back on a surfboard. Nothing was going to cloud her dreams or weaken her commitment. Does she ever think about that dark, gray, shadowy silhouette as she paddles out today? Oh, probably, but it's not enough to break her commitment to being the best surfer and accomplishing grand things in her life. In 2005, just two years after losing her arm, Bethany won her first national surfing title. She refused to be stopped. She possessed a level of commitment that declared her unstoppable.

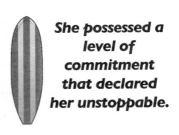

She possessed a level of commitment that declared her unstoppable.

No excuses! She did whatever it took, and that commitment took her to higher levels of results than she had previously had with two arms. How cool is that? Bethany mastered the power of momentum through a full-hearted, unwavering commitment.

HALFHEARTED COMMITMENT

But what happens when full commitment weakens to half-hearted commitment?

Surfers have an apt term for this kind of commitment. It is called "rubber arms." This term refers to surfers turning to catch a wave, making all the paddling movements, but not really going anywhere. Their minds start to weaken in focus. Surfers who have rubber arms don't really want to drop in and catch the wave. The situation may be just too intense.

In the Willis brothers' book *Discover the Greatness in You*, they say, "Many times those who practice rubber arming end up stuck at the top of the wave, getting pitched out, and experience some of the worst wipeouts possible. This is the price for not being fully committed and putting out a halfhearted effort."[3]

The true danger of rubber arms in the sales trenches is that when things get intense—you lose an account, a sure sale cancels, or that dreaded competitor swoops in and makes a better deal—it can weaken your focus to continue to do whatever it takes. Rubber arming for salespeople seeps into your preparedness, your attitude, and eventually can swallow up your mind in indifference. You're making the motions in your sales day without much willingness to stay determined in your mind. And once your mind weakens, the body always tends to follow suit.

THE REST OF THE STORY

I'm sure that at this very moment you have things you are committed to: a relationship, working out at the gym, a favorite charity. What about your mental focus? I am so grateful to have had such a patient mentor, like my former boss Julie, who took the time to help me strengthen my mental focus. In one year I learned a lifetime of lessons. Julie was so instrumental in helping me strengthen my mental toughness to cause great things to happen in my sales career. By the way, I was never moved into another territory; the company never did get new sales materials that year; and the manager in our office never left. I hit my monster numbers anyway!

As I walked across the stage that winning year to receive my National Sales Award, there stood my coach, my mentor, my boss, Julie, beaming with pride as she presented me with that stunning, fragile and breathtaking Lladro sculpture!

I pulled up in my car and took a big deep breath while walking up the driveway past the eucalyptus tree, not really sure if I was ready to recommit to the adventure sitting right in front of me. Was I going to allow the swirling of emotions and the disconnect of expectations hinder me from my own surf experience? I heard Julie's voice challenge me. If Michael never changes and Milton never wears a wristwatch, will I allow them to take away my surfing opportunity? No! Desire was back.

As I approached the garage, my eyes quickly scanned the area for any sign of the brothers. It was 10:00 a.m. exactly. Michael and Milton were nowhere in sight. But the other four young surf instructors, who looked like they were straight out of Surfer GQ magazine were there. They welcomed me with open arms and asked me to join them on the beach. Now this was a pleasant turn of events I hadn't expected.

NFL Coach Dennis Green and wife, Marie,
learn the ABCs of surfing from Milton.

Surfing has no age limits.

6

DUDE, WHERE'S THE SALE?

Top Six Momentum Breakers

Arriving at the beach with my four very hot young surf instructors, the desire to accomplish my goal of learning to surf had remarkably returned. My flight home would have to wait. I joined a family of four on the beach to begin my ocean safety lessons and to learn how to walk on water.

These young surf guides were great teachers, showing us, while we were still on the beach, our positioning on the surfboard, how to paddle out, and the technique needed to stand up when the wave was ready to carry us to the shore. Now, it was our turn. We needed to demonstrate the skill numerous times on the land while the instructors

*circled around looking for any "bad habits" that might
keep us from standing up, such as poor foot placement
on the board, leaning forward too far, or grabbing the
sides of the surfboard instead of placing palms flat on the
board as I stand up. I found myself intently focused on
my new skill set, actually enjoying becoming the student
again; pleased that I could overcome some bad habits
before they might hurt me in the water.*

Bad habits are expensive. Here's why. If you weren't lucky
enough in your young selling career to have instructors
circling around you observing and correcting your bad
habits, those habits may be costing you a lot in today's sales
trenches. They may be costing you your momentum!

Far too many of us were given some collateral pieces of
product knowledge, a map of our territory, a list of accounts,
and turned loose to just go sell. For others, it's just all too
easy to sit in sales training listening intently on the outside,
but inside be unwilling to let go of the bad habits. It's all
we've ever known. Bad habits over years and years become
our good friends—comfortable, like an old pair of sandals.
Bad habits can also keep us average and ill equipped when

the higher waves of success beckon. It's time to lose the old sandals and get off the beach!

SIX MOMENTUM BREAKERS

The real danger of bad habits is how much it costs us in terms of our energy. In chapter 3 we looked at the many ways we waste mental energy. Now it's time to look at physical energy, those areas where we spend our time in activity.

Sometimes it takes an outsider to see the bad habits that we can't. So let's look at some habits that will eventually sap your energy and rob your momentum. As you read these, circle those bad habits that might zing you—those bad habits that may have crept into your sales performance. Before we list them, here's some background on some of the habits we'll explore.

The bad habits described below come from my company's research in measuring the values we bring to this selling profession and how they impact our sales performance. Simply put, it is the "why" behind what drives us as salespeople. We move into action based on what we value. These values give us a peek behind someone's motives to perform. In using this values-and-interests assessment tool with my clients for the past ten years, I have gained a deeper insight into why salespeople perform as they do and where the potential for bad habits lurks. Sometimes our bad habits are created through overusing what we value. All of these

We move into action based upon what we value.

six values serve us in the sales field and should be respected. Each of these six values makes us special and can make or break our momentum. As I introduce the six values, ask yourself what you are the most passionate about and what drives you to perform.

1. Believing Data Sells

Doesn't it feel good to go in prepared for your sales call? Armed with research and company information is a beautiful thing, if used effectively. Too much of it can leave your customers feeling like they are drinking from a fire hose—too much too fast! This tendency to data dump seems natural for salespeople who score high in the *theoretical value*. They welcome information and are energized by data—the more the merrier. Is that you? I know many salespeople who score high in this value and leave many a blurry-eyed prospect in their wake.

STOP IT!

The brain can only handle so much data. It's time to

self-manage how you let the information flow. Here are three quick tips:

❖ **Less is more.** Choose the two most important benefits that your product or service will provide and sell those very well. Some have made the mistake in thinking that twenty benefits are more persuasive than two or three.

❖ **Number your points.** Structure your presentation the way the brain holds information. It loves a numerical, sequential flow. Anyone can lecture you for thirty minutes on why you need to automate your company's processes using their company's software and hardware solutions. Or, you can do what Roger Fallows, a senior account executive for the world's largest software company for the past twenty-six years does. His sales presentation, or demo, consists of three points:

(1) Why automate?

(2) Why now?

(3) Why his company?

The brain, when it has clarity of direction, just relaxes. Roger self-manages his information flow perfectly. He creates three buckets of information that allows the brain to focus, and then he creates a logical progression to his story.

❖ **Stop and ask.** If you know you can be tempted to data dump, make sure you are using checkpoint questions along the way to allow for the prospects to process the data you are delivering. Using questions such as "How are we doing so far?" and "Make sense?" allow your listeners to stay engaged with you.

2. Oversensing the Prospect

This bad habit has cost many salespeople the sale because of a value called the *aesthetic value.* Instead of relying on data to sell, they rely on their gut, experience, and intuition. They are emotional people who sell by "feel."

In balance, this value serves you well in reading and sensing the rhythm of the sale; however, it can be disruptive when you start overreading what the prospect is thinking, feeling, and doing. I call it Counting-the-Eye-Blinks Syndrome: You overstudy the other person and interpret what he or she is doing, down to counting eye blinks. Every movement they make is amplified in the high aesthetic's gut! Many a sale has been cut short or negotiated downward due to assuming what the prospect was thinking and feeling.

STOP IT!

For those of you with high aesthetic value, go in with your plan and stick to it. Dial down your churning stomach if prospects fold their arms or lean back in their chairs. It may have nothing to do with their interest level in your product or service. It may have everything to do with the pizza they had at lunch. Enough already! Sell from your strength and use your emotion to persuade. People always rise to your highest emotion, so sell with it—don't sell out!

3. Developing Relationships over Results

We would probably all agree that building relationships is at the heart of selling. How could we ever go wrong with valuing people? This next value if left unchecked can creep in and take us hostage if we aren't careful. It is the *social value*, which says people matter. Making a difference in the lives of people drives them. Problems start to arise, however, when we get too close to our customers at the expense of results.

STOP IT!

Marilyn, an advertising account executive, struggled every year when she had to announce to her "good friends," also known as customers, a hike in their advertising rates. She would storm into her manager's office and fight for the customer, pleading with her manager not to make her announce the rate increase. You guessed it. When we assessed Marilyn, we discovered a high social value. The social value caused her to avoid, at all costs, being seen as assertive toward her "good friends."

Business demanded the rate increase, and Marilyn had a choice to make. She had made the mistake of getting too close to customers, which affected her ability to see the business side of the relationship.

Once Marilyn understood how her values were affecting her perspective, it was time to self-manage and her creativity took over. She called me a few weeks later and explained her solution. It was brilliant!

Marilyn went into her closet and chose a special red dress.

On Monday morning during her customers' sales meeting she marched in and announced to the group: "Okay, everybody, see this red dress? This is the "advertising rates increase dress!" When I come through the door wearing this dress, you will know it's time for your rate increase!"

She's the only salesperson I know who can get people to laugh and increase their spending with her at the same time. Marilyn, you are a master! For men who rate high on social values, what if you chose a special necktie?

4. Selling by System

For some, creating systems comes naturally. These are my clients who rate high on *traditional value*, where the higher this value permeates their sales style, the more rigid they are regarding sales systems. The challenge comes when these systems, developed over the years, get in the way of adapting to the changing needs of customers.

STOP IT!

If surfers don't adapt, they die! If salespeople don't adapt, they die too! These are the people in any sales training session whose minds immediately jump to "We've already tried that" or "I've always done it this way." When this traditional value takes over, it can so easily blind us to the second right answer sitting in front of us. A revolutionary new surfing technique called tow-in surfing was unheard of until the late 1990s, when a small contingent of surfers started rethinking their systems to come up with the idea. Maybe it's time to rethink ours!

5. Wanting to Control the Sale

This one is tricky. How much control do we exercise in the sales process? Who really knows? For people with a high *individualistic value*, the answer is clear: all of it! The person with high individualistic value likes to control his or her own destiny, as well as the destiny of others.

Gene, a sales manager, had a high individualistic value and took great pride in being seen as the one in control. Can you see any problems on this sales call when he stepped through the door of the car dealership and met the general manager who also liked to be in control? His customer had just as high a need to control as Gene did, and the tension began to mount as the two started demanding control. I felt like I was a referee in the sales boxing ring!

STOP IT, before somebody gets hurt!

Know where you have flexibility and learn to move with people.

Big-wave riders learn early on that there are times to take control on the wave, and then there are times when you give up control and ride with Mother Nature—not against her. Know where you have flexibility and learn to move with people. It's a positive habit to get into.

There will be times to ask your customer for help—do it. There will be other times when you need to consider the customer's way—do it. Who knows, they might just be right!

6. The Thrill of the Kill

I have saved the most common value among salespeople for last. That is the *utilitarian value*. This is the sales engine that drives most salespeople. Simply stated, it is a drive for results. This person tends to be practical, wants a return on time and investment, and seeks results and a profession that values and rewards financial gain.

Bill Bonnstetter, CEO of TTI Performance Systems, the developer of this assessment, focused part of his research

Dude, Where's the Sale?

on the selling profession. He studied 178 top-ranked salespeople from 178 different organizations in both the United States and Germany. All of the 178 salespeople were the best that their organizations had to offer. He found that close to 80 percent of the salespeople studied had the utilitarian value as their number one value. Of course, too much of a good thing isn't always so good.

Brian has a utilitarian drive that was almost off the charts. I wanted to know how his extremely high utilitarian value affected his performance, so we met for an interview.

I found Brian to be very engaging. I discovered that his sales philosophies are right in line with what I expected: he demands the highest results from himself and settles for nothing less than being the best within his department. Brian loves to compete and enjoys the rewards of his success—financial gain. His selling style could be described in a sentence: Brian loves the thrill of the kill.

This hard-charging, successful sales professional has some bad habits though, namely, taking care of the details after the kill. Once he closes the sale, he is on to the next hunt. He sees his customers as dollar signs, a means to his financial end. Customer service after the sale is a burden and his kryptonite. Brian has lost accounts because of it. I know because I interviewed some of his customers. If you are like Brian . . .

STOP IT!

The drive for results in your career is great; wanting to be financially compensated based on your efforts is what the selling profession is all about. But when you are seduced by money and the kill at the expense of overlooking customer details, you will lose your momentum.

All of these bad habits make us vulnerable, at some level, to wasting time and energy. Self-management demands we know our habits, good and bad. How else can we manage them? I believe Lao Tse said it best; "He who knows others is learned. He who knows himself is wise."

*S*cott, one of the surfing instructors, watching me intently and checking my technique, saw no bad habits and gave me the go-ahead to hit the water with my board. He made sure my leash, a Velcro-fastened cord around my ankle, was securely attached so I wouldn't get separated from my board.

Finally, it was my turn to ride. Call me Gidget!

Learning to surf from the masters!

A California wall mural that captures the soul of surfing.

7

YOU ALWAYS GO
WHERE YOU LOOK

Discovering Impression Management

Experts make the difficult look easy. All we see, watching from the beach, are surfers, paddling with ease as the wave rises up beneath them. Then springing to their feet at just the right moment, they ride the waves of their dreams. Come on, how hard could it be?

I was surprised how easy it was to learn the Willis brothers' surfing method while on the beach. After learning the beach version, I was eager to hit the water. Well . . . hold on a minute. There is no substitute for time in the water. It's there that you learn your timing, rhythm, the feel of the wave, and how to navigate surfboard balance. It's called flow.

Paddling out into my liquid classroom, my heart was pounding out of my chest. Mentally rehearsing my brand-new surfing skills kept my focus off of the pounding waves crashing in around me. Scott helped steady my board as I lay and wait for the perfect wave to carry me to shore. Then I heard that voice . . . no not God's, but Scott's voice, yelling to me over the ocean's roar, "Eloise, go!"

I took three hard paddling motions just as I'd learned on the shore, then jumped to my feet . . . and promptly . . . fell right off the board. Headfirst! Saltwater rushed up my nose as my ankle slammed against the side of the hard, fiberglass board. Can you say "dork alert"? It was not a pretty sight.

"Okay, let's try again," Scott, shouted. We paddled out again and five more times I fell off the board every possible way, and with each fall losing any chance of ever being called cool surfer girl. It was embarrassing and I was exhausted.

Suddenly I heard a voice over my left shoulder. It was Michael, motioning for Scott to back away. Before I knew it Michael was rapidly approaching, jogging through the whitewater toward me. With the waves still pounding over *me and exhausted from failure, Michael was the last person I wanted to see! I immediately felt tense. Taking control of the situation, Michael quickly got in my face and shouted, "Eloise, where do you want to go?"*

"What kind of a question is that?" I fired back.

He repeated the question, this time with more intensity: "Eloise Owens, answer me. Where do you want to go?"

I was confused by the simplicity of the question, but at this point, I didn't have any better questions, or answers, for that matter. So I yelled back, "I want to go toward the shore, Michael!" A big "duh" echoed in my tired brain.

And then twenty-plus years of surfing wisdom came spewing from Michael's lips and broke through to my tired, frustrated brain. "If you want to go toward the shore, start looking at the shore," he said. "Every time you try to stand up, you are looking down at your feet. STOP IT! Eloise Owens, you always go where you look!"

POWER OF BALANCE

System and flow—they are the two elements that give surfers and salespeople the ability to maneuver and execute. Both are important to your sales ride. Systems give you the structure to help your prospects make great decisions. That is why I created Momentum Selling℠, a sales system designed to give you a solid foundation of skills to

❖ uncover your prospect's story
❖ persuasively tell your story
❖ influence the prospect to take action

Having a solid sales system is critical. But once you hit the sales streets or pick up the phone to use your system, you quickly realize this is only part of the process for gaining momentum. You must also find your flow.

Before we look at sales flow, don't assume that I am giving you license to ignore developing a strong sales system. I could have looked at the shore all day long and never surfed without first learning the WB Surfing system, the how-tos of surfing. You do need to master the how-tos of selling. But sometimes as salespeople we get caught up in the placement of our feet (the system) at the expense of creating a connection with the person sitting right in front of us (flow). This kind of disconnect can be extremely costly.

A colleague of mine shared a quote with me that she heard at a sales seminar: "If two people want to do business together, the details will work themselves out. But if two people don't want to do business together, the details won't make it happen." This is a great statement about flow—creating the "want" to do business together.

Lisa Kudrow, while being interviewed about her character for a television sitcom she was starring in, commented, "I loved playing someone who is oblivious to who they are and how they come across. They're completely deluded." This may make a great television show, but for salespeople it can have a devastating effect on our flow. Never forget the impact you have on the sale. Don't be deluded into believing it's all about having a superior product or an irresistible low price, because that's not always true. Unless people connect and want to do business with you, quality and price don't really matter. Here's what matters: what people think about you!

BREAKING DOWN WALLS

There is a sales phenomenon that takes place when we sell to people. I call it "the wall." If you have been in sales for any length of time, it's likely you have experienced the wall on a variety of levels.

Generally, people don't want to be sold anything, even when they have the funds to purchase a product or service. If they feel they are being talked into something, the wall of resistance goes up. Maybe your buyer has been burned by the promises of past sales reps—the wall of suspicion goes up.

The primary way we break down the wall is by managing the impressions we make with people.

Perhaps the buyer senses you are selling something you don't believe in—the wall of distrust goes up. These walls are real and get in the way of attempts to build any kind of positive flow with prospects and customers. The primary way we break down the wall is by managing the impressions we make with people. It is your personal vibe. What do people feel when they meet you?

Can we impact that? You bet we can. I call it *impression management*, the ability to influence the impressions people have when they meet and work with you. Let's take a brief look at the three elements of impression management: credibility, appearance, and environment.

IMPRESSION MANAGEMENT

As a sales coach I videotape hundreds of sales presentations every year. Without fail, salespeople are always surprised when they see themselves on tape. In part I'm looking at their sales performance and ability to demonstrate the system of selling. But that is usually not the problem. I am also looking at the sales presentation through another lens. I want to see how the intangibles are impacting the flow and connection of the sales call. The first intangible we'll explore is the power of building our credibility.

Five Dimensions of Credibility

A study was done some years ago that revealed five dimensions that give someone a high likeability or credibility score. These five credibility dimensions include:

- ❖ *Composure:* how you look and act under pressure

- ❖ *Competence:* how capable and equipped you sound

- ❖ *Sociability:* how you demonstrate social skills and manners

- ❖ *Character:* how you show your commitment to deliver on a promise

- ❖ *Extroversion:* how you demonstrate your inherent love of people

This study found that when all five dimensions come together; we have the best chance of connecting with people, or breaking down the wall, so to speak. Let's

Get off the Beach!

take a deeper look into exactly how these five credibility dimensions impact our flow.[1]

Composure. Do you know what you look like under pressure? On countless sales rides in the field, I've seen salespeople's bodies tense up, necks turn red, or their tone of voice tighten. Nonverbally we can be a walking, talking billboard for out-of-control composure, thus impacting the flow of the sale. From the hundreds of video playbacks I have observed, when the sale progresses into the money realm, it is amazing the subtle shifts salespeople make with their bodies. More often than not, salespeople subtly make a physical shift, away from the customer. What message does that send?

The ultimate in self-management is to know yourself so well that you deliberately relax your body when you know you tense up. When discussing the value and price of your products or service, you should move toward the customer, not away. You should stay cool and composed to keep your flow.

Competence. People are naturally drawn to people who can help them. Within seconds of my asking Milton a surfing question, I knew he knew his stuff. His reassuring response indicated his high competence level, and it engendered trust, which was certainly helpful, considering I was putting my life in his hands when paddling out into the ocean.

Michael Hoffman, sales trainer and president of Igniting Performance, has a favorite quote he shares with his audiences, "Trust is not how I feel about you. Trust is how I feel about me  when I do business with you." Being fully knowledgeable about all facets of your products as well as your customers' needs actually builds trust and makes your customers feel confident about doing business with you. Competence breeds trust. That's cool.

Trust is not how I feel about you. Trust is how I feel about me when I do business with you.

Sociability. Whatever happened to good, old social skills and manners in our society today? Well, if yours are rusty, then your credibility is vulnerable. I have seen flow halted over little things that can so easily become big things. Knowing how to address people, giving a strong handshake, listening and not interrupting, and showing good grooming habits all make people feel comfortable about doing business with you. Manners reflect respect for the other person and helps fuel your flow. I guess your mother was right—mind your manners and be cool.

Character. Salespeople, over the years, have unfortunately not had a great track record in the character department. Whether it was our profession at large that attracted people looking for short-term, quick sales or those who often promised what they couldn't deliver, these kinds of actions have left a bad impression in the minds of many customers and prospects. As a result, today's customers can be a bit skeptical of a salesperson's claims. Can you blame them?

We just can't afford to get close to the line of not delivering on what we promise.

Today's salespeople will always be fighting those ghosts. We just can't afford to get close to the line of not delivering on what we promise. Always deliver truth. Your honesty, even when it's tough to tell, is always cool.

Extroversion. According to the dictionary, *extroversion* is defined as "interest in and involvement with people; things outside ourselves."[2]

This definition confirms that people who are credible and likeable genuinely enjoy the people side of their profession, something outside of themselves.

But it is not enough to say you like people. How are you demonstrating it? How are you expressing it in your everyday sales walk? If there is anything that will distinguish you from the crowd with your customers, it is seeking opportunities to demonstrate your love and appreciation for people.

Impression management, as you can see from these five credibility dimensions, has a huge impact on the message you are trying to sell. Another area, our second component of impression management that also generates flow, is our appearance.

Appearance: Mirror, Mirror

What are we thinking when we get dressed for the day? Walls go up quickly with the people we meet because we forgot to pay attention to the impression of our appearance. I have been guilty as charged.

Years ago when I worked for an international seminar company, I had a full day of seminars ranging from an audience of men who worked outside climbing telephone poles for the phone company, to a small seminar for a professional women's association that met in an exclusive home in North Dallas. My schedule was tight to get from one seminar to another. Finishing up at the phone company, I dashed to my next appointment for the women's group. I raced up to the door and knocked. A very well-dressed woman, groomed impeccably answered the door and took one look at me and said abruptly, "Oh, the workers enter from the side entrance!" Then she slammed the door.

I realized immediately that I had dressed thinking about the men's audience I was speaking to and gave little thought to the women's group. My denim skirt and white blouse left a negative impression which created a wall for my next engagement. I had to dig my way out of that one and convince the hostess that this denim-dressed worker was her guest speaker. Not cool.

What about you? Have you stopped to think what impressions your wardrobe sends to people? When was the last time you stood in your closet and asked: "What fits well? What needs to be given away because I have not worn it since the Carter administration?"

Walls can go up when we undervalue the impact of our appearance.

Walls can go up when we undervalue the impact of our appearance. The appearance area of impression management is so important that I went straight to a pro for advice.

Linda Thomas, a certified image professional through the Association of Image Consultants, has become an invaluable set of "eyes" for me. She opened my eyes to the opportunity I was missing by helping me understand the power of impression I create with my appearance. Linda is a six-foot-tall redhead who knows her stuff. She started by standing in my closet then gently began to help me understand how one's closet reflects attitude and image.

In her book *My Closet, My Boutique: How to Organize Your Image*, Linda says, "When it comes to image, your closet should be a feel-good place that engages you and connects you to the next step in your successful day."[3]

Whether you are a man or woman, here are three of Linda's tips to think about as you stand in your own closet. She advises to eliminate distractions, be fashionable, and be aware of the power of color.

Eliminate the Distractions. Make sure it's easy for a person looking at you to be drawn to your eyes and maintain eye contact rather than be distracted by something negative about your clothes. Be aware of stains that you think nobody will notice or clothes that don't fit right. You want prospects talking about the great ideas and solutions you brought, not the bad impression you left.

Be Fashionable. When is the last time you invested in a good quality and fashionable piece of clothing? The key here is fashionable. Are you up-to-date on what people are wearing? If you need to update your look and don't have a lot of money to spend, I recommend investing in three things: a quality pair of shoes, a nice-looking watch with a metal band, and a well-tailored jacket. People will notice.

The Power of Color. Blue is America's favorite color. It is a dominant color in nature, it makes us happy when we see it, and it looks good on all skin tones. No wonder a large number of corporations use it in their branding logos. Here are some general color categories and their impact on people:

- ❖ Dark colors: project more authority
- ❖ Brighter colors: get attention and bring energy
- ❖ Pastels: relax and reassure people around you
- ❖ Soft neutrals, like tan: welcome and make you more approachable

Linda advises, "When getting dressed for the day, consider your day's agenda and choose the colors and clothes that will promote your goals and make you feel confident."[4]

Environment

Many a salesperson has wiped out by ignoring this final component of impression management: creating a positive, precall environment. Here is where rich opportunities await and momentum begins to break down walls. Let's look at a few examples.

Smokey Garrett, my "Realtor for Life," is a master at creating a positive presell environment. He and I met at a sales conference. I was ready to sell my home and he was eager to handle it for me. We agreed to meet. Three days before our appointment, his mystery envelope arrived in my mailbox. Inside the envelope was a folder that included the Smokey Garrett story: why his team was qualified to sell my home, a list of all of his past customers from the previous year (evidence of results), what to expect from our time together, and common questions that I might have regarding selling my home. It also included a handwritten note from Smokey confirming our time and his excitement to do business together (this was the extroversion element). Wow! He hadn't shown up yet, but already I was impressed and comfortable that I was doing business with the right team. He started to create flow before he ever showed up.

Sarah, another master of precall flow sends all her appointments an e-mail that asks them to be thinking about a question that she provides. She is not only confirming the appointment but also asking questions to get them thinking about their business in new ways before she ever shows up. By the time she arrives, the sales call is rich with discussion around her questions. She self-manages her precall flow.

My goal for you is this: When you finally walk through your customers' doors, they gladly welcome you into their day with no walls. Start building the momentum early.

It really does matter where you look and what you overlook. All these areas of impression management—credibility, appearance, and environment—are easy to overlook. But they won't be if you begin looking for them.

Could that really be true . . . that I would go where I looked? Come on, was it that important? I wondered silently as Michael steadied my board, waiting patiently for just the right wave. His voice reaffirmed what I already knew—it was my time. My arms went first, making three paddling motions to match the momentum now beginning to lift me higher up the crest of the wave. With my eyes locked on the shore, my body gingerly trying to find its balance, this time I planted my feet in their surfer stance, very naturally.

Then, on July 13, this saleswoman, mother of two, friend to many, and lover of all things ocean caught her first wave as she rode proudly, thankfully, and okay, not so gracefully toward the shore—right where she was looking!

Riding toward shore . . . right where I am looking!

8
WIPEOUTS ARE A WONDERLAND

True Lessons Waiting in Wipeouts

I had been baptized into the world of surfing, and now I was the guest of honor at the Willis brothers' backyard barbeque party. Six surfers surrounded me to welcome me into my new rite of passage. They called me EloiseOwensSurferGirl.

I was tired, sunburned, and still pretty emotional about the day. Finishing up the tasty gourmet cuisine cooked by Surfer Chef Chad, I figured it was as good a time as any to get nosey and ask my new surf brothers some questions. So while they were finishing their meal, I tenderly broached the question, "What's it like to wipe out? Has anyone here ever been hurt?" Heck, it was akin to asking a grandmother to show off her grandkids' pictures. With glee the surfers swarmed me for an impromptu show-and-tell. Immediately they all began to talk at once. With a sense of pride, Bob went first. He lifted up the left side of his tank top to show a scar on his rib cage where he had wiped out when he hit a coral reef. Chad, the youngest in the group, went next lifting his sun-bleached blond hair above his right ear to show me where he had stitches from a wipeout that tore his scalp.

Michael, now joining in the conversation, looked down at his leg and proudly displayed a scar from the leash rope that wrapped around his leg while being held under by some pretty big waves. Feeling a bit left out, I contemplated showing them the dime-size bruise on my left ankle from my own whitewater wipeout. But I refrained. My tiny bruise was no match for the wipeout wounds of the masters.

Wipeouts. Surfers can't avoid them. Fred Hemmings in the *Soul of Surfing* states, "No matter how much experience you have or how good your physical condition, on those occasions when you eat it on the big one, you are in for a rough time of it."[1]

Sales wipeouts. We can't avoid them; no matter how good we are or how long we have been selling, we can be in for a rough time of it too. The difference between surfers and us is that they aren't embarrassed by their wipeouts. We are.

When was the last time you heard a group of salespeople talking about how they screwed up the big sale and walked away empty-handed? Aren't you much more comfortable talking about the great sales you closed, hoping that you aren't outed for the ones that got away?

Do people really learn big lessons while on the mountaintop, or crest of a wave? Isn't it true that the valleys or the wipeouts are where our big lessons are waiting? The answer is yes, but only if we take time to notice and learn.

The following poem captures this point perfectly:

> The range of what we think and do
> is limited by what we fail to notice.
> And because we fail to notice
> that we fail to notice
> there is little we can do
> to change

until we notice

how failing to notice

shapes our thoughts and deeds.[2]

Studs or Students

Have you noticed that who you surround yourself with matters? It really does. Great salespeople self-manage the influences in their lives and wisely choose who they hang out with. Your energy to perform at top levels is at stake. So, who are you hanging out with? Studs or students? Let me explain the difference.

Great salespeople self-manage the influences in their lives and wisely choose who they hang out with.

Sales studs are everywhere. They can be male or female, any age, any race. They are people who steal energy by negatively influencing everyone around them. In fact, a Gallop poll survey found a bunch of them. Their survey said that some 55 percent of American workers are "disengaged." Another 19 percent are "actively disengaged," meaning that they are not just unhappy at work, but that they regularly share those feelings with colleagues.[3] They are always recruiting others to join their "elite" stud group. And believe me, it is a very popular group.

Business consultant Alan Weiss states, "Confidence is the belief that you can absolutely help others learn. Arrogance is the belief that you have nothing left to learn yourself. A thin line indeed." Sales studs have arrogance down to an art form. They are game players, rejecting any self-examination, minimizing, if not ignoring their wipeouts altogether. They would just rather complain.

Other people to consider hanging out with are those who bring you energy instead of draining it. They are called sales students, sales professionals who are always learning and not afraid to ask for help. They are teachable and not afraid to admit their wipeouts.

A colleague of mine, Chris Clarke-Epstein, past president of the National Speaker's Association (NSA), told me a compelling story about life-long students. One year while she was attending an annual NSA conference, she arrived early at one of the huge breakout sessions. She found a place right up front where she began to spread out all her note-taking stuff: her black-marbled notebook, pen, highlighter, etc. Pretty soon, another enthusiastic student took the seat right next to her. He, too, got out his learner tools, getting ready to take copious notes. As he began to spread out his materials, Chris thought he was getting dangerously close to encroaching on her study space. Feeling a bit crowded, she politely glanced up to greet this fellow learner, fully prepared to defend her turf. Suddenly she realized it was the famed sales author, Zig Ziglar, *the* Zig Ziglar. At first she thought she might be in the wrong session. Surely if Zig Ziglar, the sales motivational guru, was sitting in this session, she must be in the wrong one. But she wasn't. Chris admits she didn't remember exactly what the presenter said in that session, but whenever she saw Zig writing something down, she wrote it down too. Zig Ziglar taught her even more than the presenter did that day: we are never too old or too important to be life-long learners.

Are you choosing life-long learning? If so, it matters who you hang with.

Seek out and spend time with people who are ahead of you in ability and expertise, and be extra careful who you take advice from. Would you rather take advice from a teacher who masters whitewater's small waves, or eighty-foot monster waves? It's the difference between listening to the advice of a surfer with a bruise on her ankle from a whitewater wipeout or one with a rib cage scar who survived a twenty-foot wave in a tough coral reef environment. Listen to the people who can push you and challenge your abilities. That is how you grow and learn.

Sales students understand the importance of learning from others' mistakes (wipeouts) and self evaluate regularly. They aren't afraid to ask for help. At the conclusion of many of my sales training sessions, participants stay after for additional help. They openly share their struggle with a particular account or ask for advice, with the intent of actually using it. They're big-wave riders, students who never graduate. On the other hand, it's the sales studs who settle for little waves then brag about how well they surf them, who will never ask for help because they can never admit their wipeouts. Sales studs are missing the clarity that their wipeouts teach them. It has been said, "Where we stumble, there is our gold!" But not for sales studs; they're too busy recruiting new members to join their group.

Here are three wipeout warnings to keep you alert in your learning.

Wipeout Warning #1: Pride

Michael Willis, in his weekly column in the *Del Mar Times* wrote: "Master surfers realize they are perfect being imperfect."[4] To go after really

Master surfers realize they are perfect being imperfect.

big waves, we must grasp the humility of the task at hand. When a surfer starts thinking himself higher than the waves, the wipeouts are waiting. Don't be an egotist. Inflated self-importance shows lack of respect for the ocean and others. It's called pride.

Lise, a surf instructor, says, "There is always a wave out there better than you."

What are these surf experts trying to tell us? Pride is no respecter of persons—for surfers or salespeople. Both have egos. Egos can propel us forward through some tough obstacles, but ego can fool us into seeing only victories, thus avoiding the wisdom that awaits in our wipeouts.

Recently, I was on a sales ride with Darren, a print media sales rep, who confided that I frustrated him. Curious, I asked why.

"Because my ego tells me I am pretty good," he replied, "but your feedback is telling me differently."

Darren is a sales rep who is not making his numbers in a territory full of opportunities. His pride is blinding him to reality. Instead of pride motivating Darren to become better, it is creating a false sense of ability. What he routinely did day after day wasn't working, yet he refused to question why.

We would all rather be perfect than imperfect. But we are not. Be humble. Be open to the imperfections, study them. Here are a few questions to get you started:

- ❖ In the past year, what was your greatest wipeout?
- ❖ What did you learn from it?
- ❖ What are you doing differently today because of it?

Wipeout Warning #2: Tension

The second wipeout warning is expressed through the wisdom of another surf legend, Laird Hamilton. He states, "Tension—it is responsible for more wipeouts per day than any single known cause."

Surfers must master a term they call "calm hands." When the waves are swirling and one wrong move can send them flying into nature's washing machine on the spin cycle, it is imperative that calmness prevail.

Salespeople can be thrown into that spin cycle too, creating a tornado of tension. When left unchecked, tension can easily lure us into desperation—not exactly the most attractive thing to be wearing when you show up for your next sales call.

When I was asked to speak to a Press Association in New Jersey, they needed the seminar title and description for my two-hour program. I knew that tension was extremely high for this audience. Feeling in a feisty mood that day, I came up with a new title: "Desperate Salespeople: Five Simple Ways to Avoid Becoming One!"

My contact at the Press Association exclaimed, "I love it." So did the attendees—the session was standing-room only. I knew I had hit a nerve.

When we get desperate and tension starts penetrating

our consciousness, it can cause wipeouts without end, because desperation isn't invisible. You can see it in people's eyes and hear it in their voices.

Haven't some of our worst decisions and actions come from feeling desperate? From relationships to weight-loss diets, desperation can lure us into some pretty dumb choices. Desperation can create disastrous outcomes for salespeople as well. Customers are savvy. They can smell desperation coming a mile away and can use it to take advantage of you and your company. It can tempt us to cut profit margins or to overpromise to customers for that "desperate" sale. Can you say "wipeout"?

There is one sure way to avoid this one. Keep your new-business pipeline filled. If you get so consumed with the sales of the moment, you may not make time to develop new business waiting in your marketplaces.

Wipeout Warning #3: Timing

Surfers understand timing. They have to. There is a time to paddle and a time to stand. It isn't dependent on when you want to paddle or when you want to stand. It is all dependent on the rhythm and timing of the wave. Misread the wave and paddle too soon, and your timing is off and energy is wasted. If you paddle too late, the opportunity quickly passes you by.

Big-wave riders say that trying to predict or control Mother Nature is futile at best. She ultimately calls the shots. On their best days, surfers say they just rode what she handed them! There is no ignoring the ocean's timing.

Our customers are just like those waves and so is our marketplace, each with their own rhythm. Study your buyers' marketplace, anticipate needs, bring great ideas at just the right time, and watch your value skyrocket. Miss their timing and the opportunities can  **Miss their timing and the opportunities can pass you by.** pass you by. What's the rhythm of your buyers' marketplace? How can you use perfect timing to stand out?

They say there are only two types of surfers—those who have taken bad wipeouts and those who are going to take bad wipeouts. We are no different. I do believe there are two kinds of salespeople too—students who have the humility to admit their wipeouts and grow from them, and those studs who won't.

Always be the student.

There we stood, side by side, a most unique surf family, all bonded by the waves of the day, huddled around the last glowing embers of the backyard fire pit. Michael's voice broke the tired silence.

"Eloise Owens, you never forget who helped you catch your first wave." Michael was right. I never will!

Two Surfers and a Saleswoman

9
Position Is
Possession

Never Turn Your Back on the Marketplace

Boarding flight 1439 in the following years always promised a new adventure. This time it was the Women's Surfing Long Board World Championships at Ocean Beach. It was there that I met Kim Hamrock, a long-time friend of the Willis brothers, and a seven-time Women's National Surf Champion. She's the girl version of Milton—fearless, fun, and a freedom fighter determined to live life her way—on the waves. Her petite yet buff, well-sculpted frame could fool a casual observer. I guessed that underneath that friendly smile and untamed, wild hair was a woman who knew her destiny was out there on those waves. I guessed right!

We met and chatted briefly about the next day's events — the preliminaries, the quarterfinals, and then, for the chosen few, the finals that determined the winner.

I instantly felt comfortable with her, which probably prompted my next question: "Are the waves supposed to be good tomorrow for the competition?" The look in her eyes immediately made me realize the ignorance of my question. At first, I wanted to take it back, but the glint in her eye gave me the answer I was looking for. On many levels I totally understood.

Kim said confidently, "If the waves are pumping out there, it will be easier for me to win. But if they're not big, I'll win with what they give me." Her accountability for her performance in the next day's competition was inspiring, in a self-management sort of way.

Seven o'clock in the morning came way too early for me, but there I sat on the damp sand, sipping coffee under a blanket, trying to stay warm. The sun and the waves were a no-show. The competitors had their work cut out for them as the air horn blew, signaling the first heat of surfers to position themselves to catch the best waves they could. Women surfers from all over the world sat in the ocean, studying what Mother Nature was handing them, maneuvering for position, ready to make their move.

With overcast skies and mushy, choppy waves making their way toward shore, the women long-board participants positioned themselves toward the ocean pier, where the waves seemed to be building and breaking the best. With their wetsuits on for some help in fighting off the frigid waters, they sat on their surfboards facing the horizon, watching the wave sets approaching, adjusting to the water's tides and wind conditions. I noticed that the earliest groups were catching waves closest to the pier. As the day wore on, the take-off positions shifted. They were moving farther out to their left.

Catching great sales waves is what it's all about. Landing that big account brings salespeople such a sense of accomplishment. The pats on the back from upper management, your peers, and your family all feel pretty good. Surfers aren't fooled by a great ride. We shouldn't be

Surfers aren't fooled by a great ride.

either. In fact, surfers will tell you this very important piece of advice, which is also part of the Willis brothers' Surfer's Credo: NEVER turn your back on the ocean. Never.

Celebrate too early in the water and you'd better get ready for Mother Nature to surprise you. And I don't mean in a good way. There are new wave sets coming over your left shoulder. But you can't see them because you're too busy cashing big bonus checks.

What happens when the sales waves shift? Well, just ask Coca-Cola. As stated in the February 22, 2006, issue of *Fortune* magazine, Pepsi beat Coke in December for the first time in the 108-year rivalry, surpassing its nemesis in market capitalization. In the past, being a loser in the soda wars was the best thing to ever happen to Pepsi. It prompted Pepsi's leaders to look outside the confines of their battle with Coke. I spoke to a manager for Pepsi who believes that Coke messed up by resting on their accomplishments. "When you are number one for as long as you can remember, you assume you are doing it the right way," he said. That is, until the waves shift.

According to the *Fortune* article, what Coke investors didn't envision was the emerging wave sets coming. Gary Hemphill of Beverage Marketing observed, "They [Pepsi] were the first to recognize that the consumer was moving to noncarbonated products, and they innovated aggressively."[1] They embraced bottled water and sports drinks, going after the youth market with new edgy ad campaigns tied to the latest trends in the marketplace; that is, extreme sports, Xbox, sports figures like NASCAR's Jeff Gordon, and an affiliation with the NFL. It paid off! Never turn your back on the marketplace!

POSITION IS POSSESSION

Businesses today pay big bucks for a top online position on the Web. They want their Web site in the top position on every search engine. It's called "site optimization." This helps businesses get noticed and, hopefully, selected by potential customers. The better your position on the search engines, the more likely a prospect will find your site. Position matters. Maybe it's time we spent as much energy and resources positioning ourselves in person with our customers as we do with our Web sites.

Years ago a very powerful commercial was the talk around the water cooler. Do you remember this one?

The boss calls his whole team into the conference room and with a somber tone announces that they just lost their number one client to their competitor. The boss has airplane tickets in his hand to go visit this long-time, now ex-customer. He announces that he is headed out to go see them face to face—what they should have been doing all along but didn't. They had allowed this relationship to become common, and a competitor jumped at the chance to steal them away. They lost their position, or edge. This ad should haunt every one of us. It echoes the problem: routines are guided by the assumption that everything is a permanent condition. But to remain in top position, we need to treat everything like a temporary condition, including our customers' loyalty.

A top-of-mind position with your customers and prospects gives you incredible power as a salesperson. And here's what it takes: becoming uncommon. Try sounding like every other salesperson on the planet and see how well that works. It doesn't, especially in today's marketplace. Being uncommon gives you an edge. Uncommon can grab your customer, help you get more appointments, close more sales, and be heard above the noise.

Being uncommon gives you an edge.

Uncommon or Unconscious?

You can see this in every aspect of the world but especially in the world of branding in the marketplace. Your customers are assaulted every day by the onslaught of noise coming from businesses, all screaming for top position. As a defense mechanism, our buyers erect a force field of sorts to protect themselves from the assault. They become unconscious, in a way, switching TV stations when the commercials come, getting spam filters, opening their mail over the trash, and giving the dead man's gaze to our sales pitches. Randy Gage, a unique business consultant, makes it his life's work to push companies to explode out of the noise in the marketplace, slash through the force field, and grab their prospects by the throat. That is when momentum comes into play.

The Insanity of Sameness

What about you? How uncommon are you? Listen to my friend Randy Gage, who loves to rant over this issue of sameness.

"If you live in at least a medium-size city here in the United States, I can tell you some facts about it, even though I have never been there. You have a radio station that plays the music of the eighties, nineties, and today. One of your TV stations calls its new program *Eye Witness*

News. One station has a tagline that touts, 'Live, Local, and Late Breaking.'

"Why? Because the program director in Cleveland hears a format that works in Detroit so she rips it off. The news director in Chicago hears about something working in L.A. and immediately knocks it off.

"You have at least one electrical contractor who uses a lightning bolt on their stationary, one plumber, one dry cleaner, and one massage therapist who use the slogan, 'You've tried the rest, now try the best.' And a travel agency that gets excited about using the plane flying around the globe. I bet no one has thought of that. Sigh."[2]

Randy rants about what all of us observe every day, people who are locked into habitual, "sameness" thinking. I find them in sales companies across the nation—common approaches, common results.

Get Weird

Some years ago I was asked by a print advertising media client to kick off their "Team Excellence" week by doing a session on creativity. I think I scared them to death. My presentation was anything but ordinary. But that was okay. I wasn't there to win a popularity contest but to challenge their thinking and confront their commonness from years of sameness thinking. You could hear the ceiling fans overhead . . . whoosh, whoosh . . . as the blank stares on their faces told the true story. Changing our common routines is tough. The idea to flip from automatic pilot to mindful creativity takes energy, a bunch of energy. But the payoffs can be huge. You've got to hear this one.

Here's a story of uncommon actions and the results they can bring. Matt and his sales manager knew this sales call was going to be tough. This potential customer had a reputation for being quite demanding. They met in the lobby of the car dealership, and the general manager led them back to his office. He wasn't exactly smiling.

As they were taking their seats, the customer mentioned to Matt, in a direct, gruff sort of way, "Hey, I like that necktie."

Matt smiled.

After the sales call, Matt and his manager got back in the car feeling pretty good about reconnecting with this tough prospect. Later that day, Matt went to the local mall and got a tie box. He took off his tie and put it in the box with the note:

We hope this is the tie that binds!

The box was delivered to the car dealership and a new relationship, with a bunch of zeros attached, was born. Matt figured out how to stand out to the customer in a very memorable way for the price of a necktie.

Being creative isn't always easy but it is ultimately the

one thing that gives you the ability to claim a top position in your customer's psyche.

Beach to the Boardroom

A new breed of surfers has emerged. They see each wave as a palette to rethink surfing and develop new "air" skills. They not only catch waves, but they can also now fly over the top of the waves, seeing the waves as palettes and brush strokes on which to maneuver. It's their willingness to play on the edge that continues to push their sport.

It's important to honor what's come before, but not be limited by it.

Kelly Slater, a seven-time World Surfing Champion was asked how his creative style of surfing compared to the guys who have gone before him. "I suspect their approach was a little bit limited to their state of mind, the way they saw the waves," he said. "It's important to honor what's come before, but not be limited by it."

One surfer states, "To pull a move like this, you have to literally pick up your body and fly. A great excuse to do the same with your mind."

It's time to fly!

We can get so limited in our thinking based on what has been done before. What about redoing your fax cover sheet, rethinking your voicemail recording, creatively confirming your sales appointment, blowing up the look of your next proposal, throwing out those boooooring thank-you cards with your company logo on them, burn the holiday and birthday cards—you know, the ones that look like what your dentist sends. Here's the uncommon rule: If everyone does it, you don't! You do it differently.

OFF THE BEACH AND ON THE EDGE

What if . . . you sent fax cover sheets that are funny? Included a business cartoon, or a caricature of you?

What if . . . your voicemail caught them off guard by saying something different? What if your message was actually full of energy, instead of sounding like you're reading the obituaries on caffeine?

What if . . . when confirming your sales call appointment, you ask the customer a question about their business that you want them to think about until you arrive for the appointment? You might leave it on a voicemail message or in an e-mail.

What if . . . the first page of your common proposal is uncommon? One sales rep included on the first page of the proposal a quote from his prospect that he remembered from their initial sales meeting. The prospect called the sales rep and said, "So, you were listening." His proposal shot to the top of the stack.

What if . . . you sent Labor Day cards instead of Christmas cards? Here's my favorite idea that will absolutely get your customers laughing. One very uncommon saleswoman made it a point to remember and acknowledge her customers' birthdays but not in the usual way. She sent them a unique card on their half-birthday. So if their birthday was January 1, she sent a card on June 1. But she didn't send just any card. She cut the card in half! So they received a special card where she acknowledged their half-birthday with half a card. She sent the other half to them on their actual birthday. Uncommon rocks!

What if . . . we make a mistake and a customer's loyalty is at risk? It's no time to be common. In fact, sometimes our foul-ups are a great starting place for uncommonness to come to life. Here's one for you. This idea comes from my book *Momentum Selling: Turning Sales Breakers into Momentum Makers*, where a team of sales reps refused to lose.

In fact, sometimes our foulups are a great starting place for uncommonness to come to life.

The situation couldn't get any worse. This company messed up an already irate customer's order for the third time. Everyone in the department had written off the possibility of ever seeing a dime out of this customer again. All except one—an uncommon sales warrior who refused to lose.

She went to work on an uncommon card. Here's what it said: "We celebrate victory as a team as well as agonize over defeat. We hope you will give us one more opportunity to let us get it right. You are important to us!" Once she designed the card, she sent it around to all thirty reps in her department and asked them all to sign it. The customer, being surprised by the effort shown, gave them that one more chance.[3]

Positioning for surfers determines their success out on the waves. One surfer said it perfectly: "Willingness is not will—it's a will plus something else—something young and sorta happy to try anything, because anything might work."

For salespeople, our willingness to position ourselves through an uncommon approach opens up endless possibilities for a great sales ride. We just need to be willing to risk being weird.

Kim Hamrock didn't win the women's long-board surf competition that day. But she knew she did her best with what Mother Nature handed her. There was no agony of defeat for any of these surfers — just the pure joy of doing their best at what they love.

Do you love what you do?

Kim Hamrock, seven-time Women's
National Surf Champion, and her friend

10
STOKED!

The Three Secrets to Sales Stoke

"There is no greater feeling than standing up on a surfboard and guiding it in a jumping, sliding rush across glassy water: speed, thrills, and fun. Joy exists. You'll know it; you'll feel it."

Surfers have an apt term for it: It's called stoke. It's when the mental, physical, and spiritual side of the surfing experience all converge on the wave rider in perfect harmony. Fun meters are definitely on high. Surfers cite actually giggling out loud with pure joy. *Surfer* magazine states, "I played with the ocean today. Or maybe it was God."

SECRETS OF SALES STOKE

Salespeople, you know what that's like don't you? You were so on, so connected, riding the perfect sales wave, busting out your sales goals and hungry for more. Your momentum soars and so does your bank account. Dude, you got sales stoke!

Just like the stoke of the surfer, ours is also very mental, physical, and spiritual. And when all three of these areas converge in sync, our fun meters are definitely riding high. Joy exists. The ride is so sweet. The truth is, however, it is very easy to get out of sync and lose our stoke. It can happen to any of us. It's not like a heart attack but more like a lingering cancer that steals our stoke over time.

When we lose our stoke, we get off center, feeling inside like the sound of the washing machine when the clothes all move to one side and get unbalanced. You know—that echoing sound from the laundry room—clank-clank-thud-thud. Left unchecked, you better get ready to buy a new washing machine. The problem is, you can't pop into Sears and buy a new you! Being off center grinds you down and weakens your momentum. Surfers all agree, "When it isn't fun anymore, get out of the water!" So, how much fun are you having?

If your fun meter is on low, maybe it's time for you to

take a break, get out of the water, and sit on the beach for a bit. Let's leave the sales waves and take a minute to truly absorb this final chapter of the book. If you are reading this chapter standing in the Starbucks line for your triple latte to start your day or waiting on a client to meet you for lunch, close the book now. Read it later. The Quiet Questions you will be asked throughout this chapter will need your full attention and focus.

Let me introduce you to the three secrets of sales stoke—three areas to self-manage that will forever impact your life and how you live it forward: success is not the goal; pay attention to your pace; and people matter. Let's start with our drive for success.

SUCCESS IS NOT THE GOAL

A few years ago Barbara Walters interviewed media mogul Ted Turner. Nearing the end of the interview, she recapped his many accomplishments, such as pioneering several television networks, his ownership of a major league baseball team, and his tremendous wealth. Then after a bit of silence, moments before the interview ended, she asked her final question: "What does it feel like to be so wealthy?" In a moment of total candor, Turner responded, "It's like a paper bag. Everyone sees the bag. Everyone wants it. Once you get the bag, you discover that the bag is empty." In a rare unrehearsed moment, Turner seemed to be implying that his life looked successful but was very unfulfilled.

One of the first secrets of stoke is this: success is not the goal. In fact, success can be dangerous and addictive, just like a drug. The more you achieve it, the more you need it.

A cartoon that hangs in my office shows runners rushing full speed toward the finish line that is in complete view. The lead runner crosses the finish line in full stride. With arms raised overhead she screams at the top of her lungs, "I WIN," right before running off the cliff. I was that girl! I had to win. I was driven to succeed. Then, one night getting ready for a holiday party at the end of an exhausting year of incredible selling and finishing first . . . I passed out. The emergency room doctors poked and prodded but really couldn't find anything wrong with me. I knew. This quiet question kept racing through my mind, "Eloise, when will it be enough?" Truth is, it never is.

Would you agree with me that nothing recedes like the waves of success?

Will the results you achieve for your company today ever be enough? Probably not. It's always about more: wanting more—doing more—being more. Could this drive for more make you professionally successful yet personally empty? You bet it can. I've lived that answer. Chances are, in moments of candor, you know you have too.

Success without purpose can also overpower us and cloud the important things in life. A reporter from *The Boston Globe* interviewed former cable marketing executive Constance Barkley-Lewis on how she dealt with the loss of her job after the merger of America Online and Time Warner. "One morning I was moving the company forward, and that evening I was moving out of my office." She said that she had forgotten about her original goals and lost her focus on the things that mattered most. Listen closely. She concluded by admitting, "I hadn't lost myself when I lost my job. I'd lost myself when I found success."[1] Wow! At the top of her game she became personally empty.

Are you constantly climbing? striving? reaching? For what? And why? Where are the casualties of an unceasing, empty-bag pursuit?

Allen Tappe, a colleague and dear friend, is a master at helping people examine their own personal operating systems so they may lead a dynamic, more purposed life. In his book *The Power of Purposed Performance* he writes:

> You have to begin with what you think and believe about this life. Everything you face in life

will be defined by your own operating system. Any personal belief system will spring from the way you see yourself fitting into the world. Don't settle for a self-defining philosophy that does not respect who you are.[2]

The issue Allen so powerfully addresses is your perceived significance in this world. Do you believe you make a difference in this life? Sales stoke is born out of a passion of purpose that what you do and who you are matters. We can be successful, make a lot of money, reach a certain status, but it will be empty success, a career without fulfillment, if it's not attached to a purpose. Without purpose, you're left with an empty paper bag.

Why is that? Simply answered, we were created by God for a purpose. He designed us that way. To disregard our purpose is to deny the spiritual side of who we are. It can leave us wanting, running, and always chasing something more. Stephen Arterburn, an award-winning author, speaker, and nationally syndicated talk show host explains, "If the foundation is not exactly right, no win at the top will be able to fill the cracks at the bottom."[3] Purpose lays a foundation for us to build great things in this life . . . and keep us stoked!

Quiet Questions

1. What is your life built on?

2. What is your "why?" Why are you here?

3. Are you left holding an empty bag?

PAY ATTENTION TO YOUR PACE

One of the Willis brothers' surf rituals is going up to the top of the cliffs overlooking the mighty Pacific Ocean to watch the sunset with the surf team. It was there that Milton gently spoke: "See, Eloise Owens, even the waves rest," as he pointed to the ocean, now calm and quiet.

Are you selling in *la vida loca?* The crazy life? Jeff Conley, a colleague whose life's mission is to help people have success without starving their spirit, crossed my path years ago. I was so taken with his message that I brought him in to speak to my client's sales team. He helped me learn the second secret of sales stoke: paying attention to our pace. We all assume that to have stoke we have to speed up instead of slow down. Jeff's insights help us recognize the fault in that kind of thinking.

Standing at the back of the room, I watched this master at work. The audience laughed at his wit but was mesmerized by his message: we are suffering from speed fatigue.

Jeff states in his book *Habits of the Heart* that we are on a race for speed. Paying at the pump isn't fast enough—we need speed passes. Waiting for the microwave or ATM machines can seem like an eternity.[4]

As salespeople, depending on your product or service, all of us have seasons of intensity. Technology has turned the seasons of intensity into endless intensity. It never stops. Jeff emphasized that while engines were made to run fast, they weren't made to idle at the red line. This thirst for speed can choke our stoke! How? It suffocates our spirit and, in turn, siphons off our energy. Have you ever stopped to consider the impact of speed on your spirit? The first place to look—your energy fuel tank.

Energy is our life force. We rarely consider how much energy we are spending because we take it for granted that our energy is limitless. Then we are hit with reality. When it comes time to perform in the storm, we are out of gas. When you're really working hard, it's not easy to gauge just how run down you really are. Whose fault is that? *Ahem.* Is it your company's responsibility to make sure you rest? Your manager's? Or is it yours? How are we self-managing it? Well, judging from this next statistic, not very well.

The average full-time U.S. worker is likely to skip three vacation days this year, according to a survey by Expedia, which also found that nearly a third of employees admitted to not using all their vacation days.[5] Working 24/7 can eat us alive and steal our stoke. But why do we allow work to consume us? Consider this.

Author Elaine St. James suggests: "As long as our work is so vital that we can't slow down, we don't have to look at our own lives: a marriage that isn't working, a career that isn't satisfying, children we're out of touch with, friendships we've outgrown, or a life spiritually starved."

We just get comfortable in our chaos. We never slow down because we are too afraid of what we might see if we do.  **We never slow down because we are too afraid of what we might see if we do.**

Heck, we can't even sleep well anymore. Many studies have concluded that we are a nation of chronically sleep-deprived people. According to the research company IMS Health, consumers filled about 42 million sleeping pill prescriptions in 2005. That is up nearly 60 percent since 2000. No one can escape the media advertising for Ambien and Lunesta that experts say are needed as a side effect of an overworked, overwrought society.[6]

One article written by Lauren Winner, called "Sleep Therapy," explains that many of us trade sleep for productivity. But we would actually be more productive if we slept more. We concentrate better and are less easily distracted when well rested. Makes sense, right? Then why are we always chipping away at our sleep in order to do something else? And that something else, for most of us, is work. Read Lauren's confession and see if it doesn't feel a bit familiar.

> A simple glance at my email inbox tells me that I am not alone in sacrificing sleep in order to squeeze in a few more hours of work. Last Tuesday alone, I received 23 work-related emails that had been sent between 10:00 p.m. and 5:00 a.m. This creeped me out. The next night, in fact, I had trouble falling asleep. I lay in bed worrying about the correspondence that was accumulating in my email account.[7]

Ouch! I've been there, haven't you?

While I knew in this article that Lauren was sharing truth, it was her next point in the article that stung me the most. She makes the assertion that sleep has spiritual dimensions to it, as a demonstration of our faithfulness. She states:

> We are creatures with bodies that are finite and contingent. . . . The unarguable demands that our bodies make for sleep are a good reminder that we are mere creatures, not the Creator . . . being well rested bears witness to values higher than the cares of this world, the deceitfulness of riches, and the desire for other things.[8]

The unarguable demands that our bodies make for sleep are a good reminder that we are mere creatures, not the Creator.

She hits us between the eyes one more time by concluding, "Is it any surprise that in a society where we try to deny our mortality in countless ways, we also deny our need to sleep?"[9]

You can deny it all you want. I tried. But your body will tell the truth. Rest is not an option. Either you will do it on purpose, or eventually your body will do it for you. Choose rest, just like the ocean.

Quiet Questions

1. *When is it enough for you?*

2. *Are you resting well, or are you restless?*

3. *What happens if you slow down? Then what?*

4. *Is your body trying to tell you something now? Are you listening?*

People Matter

"The most powerful force in business isn't greed, fear, or even the raw energy of unbridled competition. The most powerful force in business is love," says Tim Sanders, author of *Love Is the Killer App.*[10] I met Tim in the hallway

Love is the infrastructure of anything worthwhile.

after a speaking engagement and found his approach to business so unusual, yet so very cool. His love definition goes like this. "Love is the act of intelligently and sensibly sharing your knowledge, networks, and compassion with your business partners."[11] Tim's fresh look at demonstrating the power of love to people who cross your path has the third secret of sales stoke written all over it.

Love is the infrastructure of anything worthwhile. It creates connections, builds rapport, and develops relationships. It feeds us mentally and physically, but most of all it fills us spiritually. Love is spiritual. It's the God-chip implanted in our hearts. We love other people because we are loved. God went first.

The challenge for us will always be not to just love but to *keep on loving*. Here's why. Because people are weird. Come on now, let's face it, we are all weird. The difference between my weirdness and yours is that I think my brand of weirdness is cool—that's all. And other people's weirdness is irritating and uncool. Just ask your kids how cool they think you are.

THE HEART OF THE MATTER

So, how well do you love the weirdness around you? How big is your heart when it deals with people much different from you? Herein lies the third secret of stoke: loving people is where it's at. *Surfing* magazine told the story of a surfer who was remembered for the size of his heart. His friends said at his funeral, "Jesse wore his love in front of him." Everyone who met him felt his love for him or her. What do people feel when they meet you?

Typically, when we lose our stoke our attitude sours

and love becomes a struggle. We aren't very patient, we get more competitive than kind, and we turn inward, selfishly grabbing to receive rather than to give. Look around.

When is the last time you demonstrated appreciation and love for the people on your team who helped you be successful?

When is the last time you demonstrated appreciation and love for the people on your team who helped you be successful? How well do you self-manage all the relationships in your sandbox? No time? Too busy? Well, I'm not buying those excuses. Interestingly, have you noticed the love fest when you meet your customers to finalize a deal or to pick up a check? I have.

How weird is it that we somehow find the energy to love on our customers, those who are writing the checks to buy our products and services, but once we head back to the office, it turns to war? I've seen sales reps treat their dogs better than they treat their support team.

Have we been duped and distracted by loving lesser things? If you can touch it with your hands and see it with your eyes, can it really be that important?

This life is about love.

Quiet Questions

1. *If your supporting team were asked to describe your feelings for them, what would they say?*

2. *Do you believe all good ideas have to come from you?*

3. *Name three people that help you be successful. When is the last time you thanked them unexpectedly? What will you do now?*

COUNTING HEADS

In December 1994, a fellow surfer sat waiting for the waves at a mystic surf break near Half Moon Bay, California. These Mavericks waves generated thick, grinding barrels tall enough to drive a bus through. Ken Bradshaw told *Outside* magazine that the waves on that Friday failed to live up to expectations. It was a little anticlimactic. Shortly before noon, however, Mavericks finally showed his face. Somebody in the gallery yelled, "Sets!" Half a mile offshore, Bradshaw saw the approaching swells and maneuvered into position. He saw Mark Foo also paddle into position and he decided to let Foo have that wave. It was the last time Bradshaw would see Mark alive.

Foo's surfboard came ashore—first in three pieces.

Bradshaw continues, "He was in the water an hour before anyone knew something was wrong." With emotion in his voice, Bradshaw said, "I just never noticed that he never came up for air." From that point on, surfing became a team sport. Now they count heads.[12]

Selling will always be a team sport. No one flies solo in success, even if you are a solo practitioner. Every day, you come in contact with people who help you succeed. They might be vendors, customers, or the letter carrier who delivers your mail. So, who is on your team? How connected are you to them? Do you care? Better yet, do they know you care?

THE POWER CONNECTION

Before every surf lesson, the Willis brothers call for a power circle. Those on the beach, young and old, waiting to learn to walk on water know that something special is about to happen. All those in the group circle up and, instead of holding hands, everyone is joined knuckles to knuckles. Not sure what to expect in my first power circle, I curiously listened. They explained that we are all connected to each other—a circle of energy—

and it makes our time together special. We learn as a group, we succeed as a group, and we end the day as a group. Following our surf class, the power circle was called again and each person was asked, while standing knuckles to knuckles, what they learned out in the water. It was amazing how connected I felt to those in the circle. We celebrated when we saw each other stand up and encouraged each other to try again when we wiped out. Believe me, I received a lot of encouragement!

But at the end of the day, we were a team and we counted heads.

Maybe it's time you counted heads to see how well everyone is doing in your circle of success. Maybe it's time to thank them unexpectedly, to sacrifice willingly, to demonstrate patience, and to value their differences, respectfully. Really, just love them.

ENJOY THE RIDE

According to Michael Willis, the best surfer in the world is the one having the most fun!

Let's simplify things. It takes great balance to surf. It takes great balance to live. Both professional salespeople and surfers will probably always struggle with navigating just the right kind of balance every time, every day. So why not just give this life your best attempt by building your life on things that matter and fill you with purpose. By learning the lessons of the waves and making time to rest, really rest. By making absolutely sure that you wear your love in front of you, demonstrating love to all who cross your path.

Life will feel more full again. The momentum to step out of your regular results and step up to higher waves of success will lay new opportunities at your feet. And most of all, you will become the best surfer in the world—the one having the most fun.

Now, GET OFF THE BEACH! . . . and enjoy the ride!

Notes

Chapter 4: Will You Surf or Go Home?
1. Andy Martin, *Walking on Water* (London: John Murray Publishers, 1991), 73.

Chapter 5: Facing Monster Waves
1. Brennan Manning, *Abba's Child: The Cry of the Heart for Intimate Belonging* (Colorado Springs, CO: Navpress, 2002), n.p.
2. Milton and Michael Willis, *Become a Surfer: The ABC's of Surfing* (2002). Available online at www.wbsurfing.com/willis/Products/ ebook.html.
3. Milton and Michael Willis, *Discover the Greatness in You* (Boulder, CO: Blue Mountain Press, 2006), n.p.

Chapter 7: You Go Where You Look
1. McCroskey, Holdrige, and Toomb, "Five Dimensions of Credibility," Empirical Research, University of Houston, 1974.
2. *Encarta World English Dictionary,* www.encarta.com, s.v. "Extroversion."
3. Linda Thomas, *My Closet, My Boutique: How to Organize Your Image* (Dallas: LNP Publishing, 2003), n.p.
4. Thomas, *My Closet, My Boutique.*

Chapter 8: Wipeouts Are a Wonderland
1. Fred Hemmings, *Soul of Surfing* (New York: Thunder's Mouth Press, 1997), n.p.
2. Daniel Goleman *Vital Lies, Simple Truths: The Psychology of Self Deception* (New York: Simon & Schuster, 1996), 24.
3. Jim Loehr, Tony Schwartz, *The Power of Full Engagement* (New York: Simon & Schuster, 2003), n.p.
4. Michael Willis, Inside Surfing, *Del Mar Times,* April 2005.

Chapter 9: Position Is Possession

1. Katrina Brooker, "How Pepsi Outgunned Coke," *Fortune*, February 1, 2006.
2. Randy Gage, Randy's Rants, www.randygage.com, April 2005.
3. Eloise Owens, *Momentum Selling: Turning Sales Breakers into Momentum Makers* (2004), 23.

Chapter 10: Stoked!

1. Constance Barkley-Lewis, "Magazine Addresses Employees' Inner Needs," *Worthwhile*, as reported in *The Boston Globe*, 2006.
2. Allen Tappe, *The Power of Purposed Performance* (Arlington, TX: Institute for Purposed Performance, 2003), 2. Used by permission.
3. Stephen Arterburn, as quoted in Jeff Conley, *Habits of the Heart* (Newberg, OR: Book Partners, 1999), 25.
4. Conley, *Habits of the Heart*, 140.
5. Annual Survey, Expedia, as quoted in *Star-Telegram*, 2006.
6. Stephanie Saul, "Lifestyles boosting sales of sleep aids," *Star-Telegram*, 2006.
7. Lauren F. Winner, "Sleep Therapy," Christian Vision Project, 2006.
8. Winner, "Sleep Therapy."
9. Winner, "Sleep Therapy."
10. Tim Sanders, *Love Is the Killer App* (New York: Three Rivers Press, 2003), n.p.
11. Sanders, *Love Is the Killer App*, n.p.
12. Jon Krakauer, "Mark Foo's Last Ride," *Outside*, May 1995.

About the Author

Eloise Owens walks her sales talk. An award-winning National Sales Professional who writes and speaks from twenty years' experience in the sales trenches, she is the creator of Momentum Selling℠, an innovative training system that gives sales organizations uncommon ways to sell and service their customers.

She has been quoted in national sales publications including *Selling Power* magazine, which interviewed her on the power of momentum within sales organizations and the impact it can have on results.

Since 1991, clients such as Hilton Hotels, State Farm Insurance, Ericsson, Norwegian Cruise Lines, and Parke-Davis Pharmaceuticals have called her their "Momentum Maker."

Eloise's momentous touch has inspired hundreds of sales professionals not to wait for momentum but to go create it! She lives in Dallas and has two children who have both graduated and are actually employed!

To obtain information on Eloise's presentations, seminars, or volume discounts for *Get off the Beach!* contact her at

The Momentum Company

972-956-9366

Eloise@momentumcompany.com

www.MomentumCompany.com

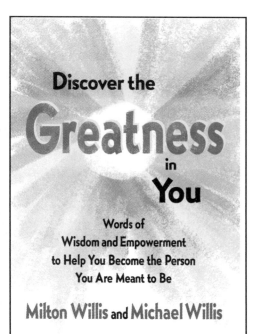

Discover the
Greatness
in
You

Words of
Wisdom and Empowerment
to Help You Become the Person
You Are Meant to Be

Milton Willis and Michael Willis

Discover the Greatness in You

The Willis brothers use the skills and knowledge they've learned surfing the world's largest waves to show you how you can develop the willpower to win, achieve a lifetime dream, and exceed all expectations. With their compelling words of wisdom, they challenge you to discover your own greatness and become the person you are meant to be.

ISBN 1-59842-069-0

Also available through the
Willis brothers' Web site:
www.wbsurfing.com

Discover the Greatness in You

Available from

Blue Mountain Arts

P. O. Box 4549
Boulder, CO 80306
800-525-0642 / 303-449-0536
Fax: 800-545-8573 / 303-417-6496
E-mail: bmaorder@sps.com
www.sps.com